W9-BVK-499

libertarianism,

from

to

libertarianism,

from

to

JEFFREY A. MIRON

BASIC
BOOKS

A Member of the Perseus Books Group

New York

Editorial production by *Marra*thon Production Services, www.marrathon.net.

Design by Jane Raese
Text set in 10.5-point ITC Century Book

Library of Congress Cataloging-in-Publication Data is available for this book.
ISBN 978-0-465-01943-4

10 9 8 7 6 5 4 3 2 1

To the memories of

Milton Friedman,
Bob Rosenthal, and
Bernie Saffran

contents

D

E

F

G

H

I

L

M

W

Z

preface

When I first arrived in the Department of Economics at Harvard University for a visiting position for the 2004/2005 academic year, I asked what courses the department wanted me to teach. The happy answer was, "Something about your own stuff." I wasn't exactly sure what that meant, but I took it as an opportunity to think through my economic and political views on a broad range of issues. The course that emerged was "A Libertarian Perspective on Economic and Social Policy." The lecture notes from that course became the first draft of this book.

My interest in libertarianism developed late in life, although it may have been preordained. I entered Swarthmore College in 1975 planning to major in French and become a lawyer but enrolled in introductory economics during my first semester to fulfill Swarthmore's distribution requirements. It took just one class for me to realize I had found my calling. Economics seemed elegant and interesting, and it provided a way to think consistently—but not foolishly—about a variety of topics and ideas. At the time I focused more on the discipline's mathematical clarity than on its role in policy analysis, but its laissez-faire implications also resonated.

When I moved on to graduate school in the economics department at the Massachusetts Institute of Technology in 1979, my research addressed macroeconomic topics like interest rates, monetary policy, and economic stabilization. While these topics include policy questions, to be sure, they're not the ones traditionally associated with libertarianism or free-market economics. And so my interest in the libertarian perspective on policy remained dormant.

In 1988, while I was on sabbatical at the National Bureau of Economic Research in Cambridge, Massachusetts, the bureau began a project to study the economics of illegal drugs. The project addressed such questions as the price elasticity of demand for drugs (that is, how does the demand for drugs respond to changes in the price) and the industrial organization of drug markets (the relationships among growers, processors, dealers, and users)—standard economics fare. Out of curiosity I sat in on these early discussions and was struck that no one seemed curious as to why, exactly, marijuana, cocaine, and heroin should be illegal when alcohol was not. Some initial investigation suggested that most arguments for prohibition were not convincing or based on flimsy evidence, so I undertook several research projects that evaluated the wisdom of drug prohibition. Within a short time this work convinced me that legalization made more sense than prohibition; here was the doorway to my libertarianism.

At one point during this period an economist who shared my views on drug legalization said something like, "Of course, you're not one of those nuts who supports legal gun ownership, are you?" I had not given the question much thought, but I realized immediately that many arguments for legalizing drugs apply with equal force to guns. So, I told him, in effect, yes, I was one of those "nuts." And I realized that I needed to think through my views on a range of issues, if I was going to be consistent. Fortuitously, I began writing op-eds for the *Boston Herald* and the *Boston Business Journal* around the same time, which provided me the opportunity to consider new topics such as education, poverty, and taxation. I generally concluded that small government is the right approach.

Teaching my Libertarianism course at Harvard was the perfect opportunity to undertake a full-scale evaluation of the role of government in modern society. It also provided me with the chance to try out my perspective on a critical audience. I learned a great deal from the student reaction to my views, and, after teaching the class a second time, I decided to convert the lecture notes into a book. This was more difficult than I anticipated, and I regularly cursed the day I signed the book contract. After making an abortive attempt at a book organized traditionally in chapters and poorly suited to either an academic or lay audience, I stumbled on the idea of the dictionary format, and this approach flowed (somewhat) more easily. Now with the agony of writing behind me, I hope that putting my thoughts into print has made them more consistent and understandable, whether or not more persuasive.

My intellectual debts to teachers, colleagues, and friends are innumerable. All these people influenced this book in one way or another, even though many do not share my views on policy.

My undergraduate economics training could not have been more rewarding. Howard Pack, my first economics professor, convinced me in a heartbeat that economics was the subject for me. Rob Hollister's course in econometrics inspired me to think carefully about what we can learn from data. Mark Kuperberg warned me that while microeconomics had good answers, macroeconomics had good questions. The late Bernie Saffran's insistence on arguments and evidence, not assertion, is perhaps the most important lesson I learned in any course. "I am willing to be wrong," Bernie would say, "but I need to be convinced." I would not be an economist today were it not for Bernie, and his economic theory seminar was the most rewarding experience of my undergraduate career. The discussion in this class also presaged my future views on policy. In one session a fellow participant and I argued that women should be legally allowed to sell their babies, a position that brought one classmate to tears.

I am indebted to my mentors in graduate school for their teaching and advice, even though none shares my perspective on policy. Stan Fischer was a superb advisor and a good friend. He inadvertently contributed to my libertarianism by bringing me with him as a research assistant during his sabbatical at the Hoover Institution in 1981, giving me a chance to hear Milton Friedman, George Stigler, and other free-market economists firsthand. Larry Summers, Olivier Blanchard, Julio Rotemberg, and the late Rudi Dornbusch all taught me to respect both theory and evidence, which I hope makes me a better economist.

My colleagues at the University of Michigan and Boston University, where I taught before moving to Harvard, suffered my frequent rants about libertarianism and helped make my views more intelligible. These colleagues also provided the kind of friendship crucial to a productive environment. I thank especially Bob Barsky, David Lam, Jeff Mackie-Mason, Gary Solon, John Bound, Severin Borenstein, Donald Deere, Michael Salinger, Jim Levinsohn, Paul Courant, Miles Kimball, Matthew Shapiro, Kevin Lang, John Leahy, Larry Kotlikoff, Michael Riordan, Raquel Fernandez, Paul Beaudry, Andy Weiss, Bart Lipmann, Jon Eaton, Russell Cooper, Simon Gilchrist, Eli Berman, Hsueh-Ling Hyunh, Debraj Ray, Michael Manove, Alwyn Young, Debby Minehart, and the late Bob Rosenthal.

The students who took my Libertarianism course at Harvard made it a memorable experience and thereby encouraged me to write this book. I am indebted in particular to Mike Kopko, Elina Tetelbaum, Michael James, Dan Obus, Elizabeth Rhinesmith, Sarah Maxwell, Vivek Ramaswamy, Joseph Carrubba, Kevin Cleary, John Durant, Ryan Fawaz, David Kirby, Matthew Knowles, Brian Kozlowski, Jeff Miller, Sarah Milov, Craig Sincock, Alice Chen, Daniel Robinson, Andrea Ellwood, Grace Hou, Sarah Miller, Sarah Paiji, Allison Rone, Joshua Samuelson, Greg Michnikov, Ravi Mehta, Jenny Skelton, Alex Harris, Eugen Taso, Jason Yeo, Robert Cecot, Erik Lawler, Christopher Altchek, Daniel Robinson, and Michael Steinhaus.

I am grateful to Angela Dills, Jeff Zwiebel, and Elina Tetelbaum, who co-authored research that underlies some of the material presented here.

Numerous friends, relatives, and colleagues at large helped me think through my policy views. I am grateful in particular to Fady Khairallah, Chris Bradley, Karim Sahyoun, Todd Hoffman, Dan Murphy, John Summers, Anita Tien, Ralph Minehart, Jean Minehart, Ken Bellerose, Beth Minehart, Eric Biedermann, Debby Minehart, John Rust, Sara Bloom, Laird Bloom, Doug Miron, David Weil, Ed Glaeser, and Steve Zeldes. Fady Khairallah, Karim Sahyoun, Anita Tien, Ralph Minehart, Laura Miron, Alex Tabarrok, and Greg Mankiw also read drafts and made invaluable suggestions and corrections. I cannot thank these people enough for their insightful comments.

The Harvard Department of Economics has been an amazingly warm and friendly environment in which to think about libertarianism. Alberto Alesina, who first invited me to visit the department, and Jim Stock, who made my continued stay at Harvard possible, deserve special mention. Although few members of the department share my libertarian perspective in whole or even in part, they have all tolerated my views and, I think, enjoyed pushing me to defend more and more extreme positions. While occasionally this made me feel stupid, I hope it ultimately sharpened my analysis.

I am especially indebted to Greg Mankiw. He has taught me economics for more than 25 years, served as a constant foil for my wacky views, and been a true friend to boot.

I thank Tim Sullivan of Basic Books for his interest in this project and his tireless editing.

My parents provided an atmosphere growing up that undoubtedly contributed to the views I hold today. Our dinner table was a friendly debate society, and I relish few things as much as a good argument. This environment also instilled in me an unwillingness to accept conventional wisdom, and it might explain why many consider me cynical about politics (I think I'm just being realistic). My father's own libertarianism, instilled when he was a law student in the 1950s at the University of Chicago, lay dormant for many years but gradually bubbled up and exerted a lasting influence.

Finally, I thank my wife, Patty, my daughter, Laura, and my son, Daniel. They have suffered my libertarian babblings for many years and occasionally conceded some merit in my views (while we were dating, Patty opined, before knowing

my politics, that prostitution should be legal). Most impor-
tantly, my family has been supportive in every conceivable
way. I would never have finished the book without their faith
and encouragement.

libertarianism,

from

to

introduction

What is the appropriate size and scope of government? Liberals and conservatives offer radically different perspectives on this question, but both advocate big government in many areas. Roughly, liberals support economic regulation while conservatives favor social and foreign policy intervention.

Libertarianism argues for limited government across the board. In broad brush, libertarianism is socially liberal and fiscally conservative, so libertarians want government out of people's bedrooms and out of their wallets. This description hides a host of more subtle issues, since balancing the pros and cons of different policies is often not trivial. Thoughtful application of the libertarian perspective nevertheless leads to consistent conclusions about which parts of government are beneficial, and which are not.

The principles of libertarianism point toward legalizing drugs and prostitution, replacing public schools with vouchers, and eliminating farm subsidies, trade restrictions, and middle-class entitlements. Libertarianism opposes regulation of guns, child labor, campaign finance, unions, financial markets, and more. Libertarianism would leave abortion policy to state governments, terminate foreign policy interventions, and get government out of the marriage business. Under libertarianism, government would take part in national defense, criminal justice, and contract enforcement, but little else.

These positions rely on the idea that, however well-intentioned, government often does more harm than good. Most government generates more cost than benefit because interventions fail to achieve their stated goals and even create unintended consequences, many far worse than the imperfections these interventions were intended to fix. Private arrangements, on the other hand, work better than many people recognize, and imperfections in one private arrangement give rise to others that dampen the harmful effects of the first (and so on) in an ever-evolving, robust system. Markets aren't perfect; they have to adjust over time and may have inefficiencies. But government is worse.

Libertarianism, from A to Z analyzes existing and proposed government policy in three steps. It first asks whether, in a given arena, the problem that allegedly justifies government intervention is substantial and whether private arrangements might significantly ameliorate it, if a problem exists in the first place. Next, *Libertarianism* addresses whether, in cases where private mechanisms seem genuinely insufficient, proposed interventions for the problem achieve their stated aims. *Libertarianism* then considers the positive and negative consequences of the proposed intervention, including its unwanted side effects as well as its direct costs. *Libertarianism* advocates intervention if, but only if, the entire set of consequences from intervention is better than from laissez-faire, meaning a policy of non-intervention.

I call this approach "consequential libertarianism" because it draws conclusions based on what effects different policies have on the economy and society. This approach differs from the brand of libertarianism called philosophical, or rights-based, which invokes particular principles about liberty or property rights as the basis for choosing between policies (see **consequential versus philosophical libertarianism**). The consequential approach is, fundamentally, just the insistence that appropriate evaluations of competing policies must consider all their effects, not just a subset or the stated intentions.

This approach to analyzing policy should not be controversial—but it is. Some worry that the libertarian approach leaves no room for considerations of morality or social justice, but this concern is misplaced. Terms like "morality" and "justice" are just shorthand for consequences that are widely regarded as undesirable. For example, the view that war is immoral is really a consequential conclusion that war causes death and destruction without beneficial impacts that outweigh the harms. Morality and justice fit in the consequential framework just fine, because the approach makes explicit the consequences that underlie views about morality, justice, and similar values.

The potential difficulty with consequentialism isn't the issue of justice but that policy decisions involve tradeoffs. Every private arrangement is imperfect in some way, while every government policy generates positive and negative effects. So, accepting the consequentialist approach might not seem to settle any issues. To make matters more difficult, some consequences of policy are difficult to quantify, and people hold disparate views about which consequences deserve the greatest weight in policy evaluations. It might seem, in fact, that one can accept the consequentialist perspective and yet disagree radically with the specific conclusions derived in this book.

Where does that leave us? The libertarian claim, which *Libertarianism, from A to Z* attempts to substantiate, is that most policies have so many negatives, and private arrangements are sufficiently good, that radical reductions in government make sense for any plausible assessment of the effects of most policies and for any reasonable balancing of these effects. This assessment does not apply in every case; libertarianism accepts a role for government in a few, limited areas: small government, not anarchy. But these interventions—in national defense, criminal justice, and contract enforcement—are the exceptions to the rule.

Libertarianism, from A to Z presents the case for libertarian policy conclusions in a series of short essays about government policies and related issues. This format is meant to make the discussion accessible to a broad audience and to avoid excessive detail when possible. It also aims to help you learn to think like a Libertarian, by applying broad principles systematically and consistently across a broad range of issues. For example, a number of essays explain that state-level intervention is less bad than federal intervention, even if the state interventions are themselves undesirable, because a state-by-state approach allows variety and experimentation that help identify the positive and negative effects of policies.

The ordering of the entries is alphabetical, for want of a better alternative. Each entry is meant to be self-contained, but all of the entries rely upon pursuing the same logical course. One key aspect of libertarianism is its consistency in applying a skeptical view to all policies, so ideas that arise in one area spill naturally over to others.

The selection of entries is not meant to be all-inclusive, and I've intentionally erred on the side of fewer with the hope that general principles emerge clearly enough. There are several kinds of entries: those that discuss general policies (**anti-poverty programs**), those that discuss specific policies (the **Civil Rights Act of 1964**), those that discuss relevant historical episodes (the **Great Depression**), those that discuss ideas related to libertarianism (**utilitarianism**), and so forth. Many entries contain cross-references to related entries in the form of a "see also" line.

The discussion focuses on policies that involve large-scale government expenditures, that affect large sectors of the economy and society, and that illustrate key adverse effects of government interventions. Federal policies get more attention than state policies, since federal interventions do more harm. Quantitatively important policies receive greater scrutiny than policies that, however ill-conceived, do not affect many people. The analysis also focuses on the key issues in modern political debates: education, poverty, and discrimination, but also abortion, gay marriage, national security, and campaign finance. The analysis shows that consequentialism consistently evaluates policies based on their effects, not on preconceived assumptions about when intervention is beneficial or how good it might make us feel.

The tone of the analysis is part advocacy, part explanation. While the discussion attempts to make the best possible case for libertarian conclusions, the book aims to provide a balanced introduction to libertarianism for readers who want to understand the libertarian view, whether or not they find it convincing. This book tries both to indicate in a concise way what the standard libertarian positions are and to outline the main reasons for those positions.

The phrase "libertarian position" is, of course, a simplification. Just as those who consider themselves liberals or conservatives often disagree with their fellow travelers, libertarians differ not infrequently on key issues. Indeed, some libertarians will object vehemently to a few of the conclusions offered here (see, for example, **gold standard versus fiat money**). But libertarians unquestionably share a broad, common core of judgments about the appropriate size and scope of government, so it makes sense overall to talk about "the" libertarian perspective.

I hope that *Libertarianism* will, if nothing else, inspire readers to think and talk clearly and honestly about the role of government in society. I am confident that when this happens, policies get better.

abortion

Opponents regard abortion as murder and want to ban it, while defenders view abortion as a fundamental privacy right and resist most or all legal restrictions.

The standard argument for banning abortion assumes that human life begins at conception, a view that implies that abortion is murder. Since governments prohibit murder, it seems to follow that governments should prohibit abortion.

The "abortion is murder" view is understandable, but it is not decisive. If the pregnancy is successful, a fetus becomes a person, but few people regard a fetus as identical to a person, and determining when human life begins is colored by moral, emotional, and religious considerations. Taking the next step in the position, defining life as beginning when a fetus becomes "viable" (that is, able to live outside the uterus) is vague, in part because the point of viability is constantly evolving.

Beyond the difficulty of defining when life begins, both law and morality recognize legitimate reasons to take life. Examples include self-defense, the death penalty, and the shooting of suspects by police. In all these cases, society's judgment is that while taking a life is undesirable, the positives outweigh the negatives. That is, society takes a **consequentialist** approach—it balances pros and cons—in deciding when the taking of a life is acceptable.

Thus, even if a fetus is a human life, abortion should be morally tolerable if the benefits of terminating a pregnancy exceed the negatives, taking into account the impact on the pregnant woman, her existing and future children, and society generally. Further, abortion should be legal if outlawing abortion imposes adverse consequences that are worse than those associated with terminating unborn fetuses. The question, therefore, is what costs arise from banning abortion.

The first problem is that while bans probably reduce the frequency of abortion, they are only partially effective. Some women obtain legal abortions in other states and countries or from doctors who exploit ill-defined areas in the law (such as exceptions for protecting the mental health of the mother). Other women obtain abortions from back-alley providers or by using coat hangers or toxic substances.

The fact that a law is imperfectly enforced is not by itself reason to eschew it. No society catches every murderer, rapist, or thief, yet no one argues for legalizing such actions. Banning abortion is different than banning murder, however; virtually everyone agrees murder is wrong, but many regard at least some abortions as acceptable. This implies a number of negatives from bans.

These negatives include increases in the health risk for women who obtain abortions despite the ban. Some abortion opponents place little weight on the welfare of such women, regarding them as murderers, but that is an extreme view. Many abortion opponents claim that abortions harm the women who have them, not just the unborn fetuses. By driving abortions into the black market, or preventing abortions where a birth has serious negatives for the woman, outlawing abortion harms some of those the ban allegedly aims to help.

As with any law that is difficult to enforce, an abortion ban generates **disrespect for the law** from those who obtain black market abortions or convince doctors that an abortion is essential for a mother's health. A ban enriches doctors who exploit gray areas in the law relative to those who obey the spirit of the law. Bans also allow women of means to retain access by traveling to countries where abortion is legal, while the poor face greater obstacles, so bans have a disproportionate impact depending on one's income.

Abortion bans can also harm pregnant women and others, even when they reduce abortion. Some women desire abortions because they lack the physical or emotional resources to care for a child, or because they believe an additional child will hurt their existing family. The pregnancies not terminated due to an abortion ban can produce children who are especially likely to experience unfavorable life outcomes or impose welfare or medical costs on society.

Any attempt to enforce an abortion ban intrudes into the relationship between a woman and a man or between a woman and her doctor. More broadly, abortion bans endorse the view that governments have the right to control what people do with their own bodies. If followed to its end, this implies that governments can jail pregnant women who drink alcohol or eat junk food, since this might harm the fetus. This view also suggests that governments can prohibit drugs, ban subversive books, or mandate exercise and religion.

One can therefore mount serious arguments against abortion bans, even if a fetus is a person. If human life begins sometime during gestation, the case against bans is even stronger since the argument that abortion is murder would not apply to early-term abortions.

The fact that bans are bad policy does not prove that all restrictions on abortion are undesirable. Laws that limit late-term abortion have fewer adverse effects than total bans, and they target the abortions most likely to generate moral or ethical concerns. Determining the correct dividing line for legal abortion, however, is difficult.

A natural way to balance different views on abortion is to leave abortion policy to lower levels of government. In the United States, this means overturning the Supreme Court's *Roe v. Wade* decision and letting each state determine its own abortion policy, free of federal restriction or compulsion. Past experience suggests most states would allow legal abortion to some degree, yet the anger felt by those who oppose abortion would be muted. And even strict bans on abortions would have less impact because they would affect a smaller population.

See also **federalism, partial-birth abortion, RU-486.**

accountability and high-stakes testing

Due to concerns about the quality of **public schools**, education reformers in the 1990s turned to an approach known as accountability, a system that requires public school students at various grade levels to sit for "high-stakes" tests in math, English, and other subjects. Governments publish the results, which lets parents and administrators know which schools are performing well. The tests are "high-stakes" because they sometimes determine whether students can graduate and also carry rewards or punishments for teachers, principals, and schools, such as the amount of funding received by a school district.

Advocates of accountability make two arguments for this approach to improving public schools. First, results from the high-stakes tests allow parents to compare schools and then vote with their feet, thereby pressuring bad schools to improve. Second, the rewards and punishments incurred by low-performing students and schools generate more studying, better teaching, increased attention to curricula, and so on.

This sounds good in principle, but the reality is less impressive. Accountability has always been present to some degree because motivated parents locate in better school districts or send their kids to private schools, which is why the glaring deficiencies of public schools are largely absent in middle- and upper-income neighborhoods. Poor educational outcomes occur mainly in low-income neighborhoods, where parents cannot move away from a bad public school or afford a private one. Accountability, however, does not provide any additional choice for low-income parents. The fundamental problem at low-performing schools, moreover, is that family support for educational achievement is often absent, a problem accountability also fails to address.

In some instances, better ways of running schools are available but are not being used. For example, many schools suffer from inflexible hiring and firing rules imposed by unions, or from outdated or misguided curricula. Also consider that although the results of high-stakes tests can indicate where educational performance does not meet reasonable standards, this information does not provide a mechanism for change.

The test score improvements that result from high-stakes testing, moreover, must be interpreted with caution. Higher test scores might reflect greater learning, but they can also result from increased classification of students as learning disabled or non-English-proficient, from cheating by students and teachers, and from increased teaching of test-specific skills that have little value outside the context of the test. Increases in test scores on the subjects tested, such as math and English, can result from reduced attention to areas not tested, such as science; likewise, increases can reflect learning that is short-term or not broadly applicable, rather than translating into long-term benefits such as broader skills, improved graduation rates, or higher income later in life.

A further problem is that accountability creates a focus on students in the lower part of the test score distribution, since raising the pass rates of underperforming students is the standard way high-stakes tests are used to allocate funding or impose punishments on low-performing schools. This likely harms students above the passing score by dumbing down the curriculum.

Perhaps the greatest problem with the accountability approach is that it imposes one kind of education—a narrow focus on test scores—on everyone. If tests are well-designed, then higher performance is presumably better than lower performance, but quality schooling is not just about test scores. A well-designed system matches students to appropriate programs such as college prep for some and vocational training for others. Good schooling introduces students to new ideas, inspires them to be critical thinkers, and instills an interest in learning. Accountability asserts that the same program, one focused rigidly on test scores, is right for everyone.

Accountability is also problematic because it seems to provide a fix at no cost and thereby distracts attention from more fundamental reforms—**vouchers** and elimination of teachers' **unions**—that would do far more to improve the quality of government-funded education.

See also **subsidizing education.**

affirmative action

The United States and other countries use affirmation action in an effort to reduce **discrimination**. The exact definition of affirmative action varies widely and is the subject of much debate. One variation in the policy includes advertising job openings especially to members of a targeted group. Another version is setting a lower bar for performance on a qualifying exam, as occurs in police hiring in some cities. A further example is adopting more flexible interpretations of the appropriate qualifications for university admission, such as de-emphasizing test scores and putting more weight on community service or extracurricular activities. Still another is requiring banks to make mortgage loans in minority neighborhoods.

The usual justification for affirmative action has two components: the claim that discrimination would be widespread in the absence of government attempts to prevent it, and the claim that **bans on discrimination** do not provide a substantial check on discrimination.

The second claim is indisputable. Any decision to hire, promote, lend, or admit reflects numerous considerations, so judges and juries can rarely know the true motives of an alleged discriminator. Thus, if anti-discrimination policy consists merely of laws that ban discrimination, and if these laws require evidence that a particular employer, bank, or school has discriminated against a specific person, then courts will rarely convict anyone of discrimination. A society that wants its discrimination bans to have teeth must therefore impose affirmative action, since these policies are more readily enforced.

But affirmative action generates its own costs, regardless of the magnitude of discrimination that would otherwise occur.

First, affirmative action diminishes the accomplishments of women and minorities who can succeed without government help. In the absence of affirmative action, the achievements of these groups would attest to their determination and talent. History provides innumerable examples of women and minorities who succeeded despite discrimination. Under affirmative action, however, some people believe that success by these groups results from affirmative action rather than merit. This belief is understandable, moreover, if affirmative action sometimes produces favorable treatment of people who are not necessarily the most qualified.

Affirmative action can also breed resentment against the targeted group from persons who believe they have been unfairly passed over because of affirmative action policies. In many cases this belief is erroneous, but affirmative action still gives those with tendencies toward prejudice a personal and emotional basis for even stronger discriminatory views.

Affirmative action diverts attention from private actions that women and minorities can take to overcome discrimination, such as acquiring extra education or putting forth extra effort. It might seem unfair that persons subject to discrimination should have to work harder to get what they deserve, but at least these efforts benefit other members of the protected group by breaking down barriers and avoiding any implication of special treatment.

Under affirmative action, persons who believe they will receive preferential treatment might assume that education and hard work are unnecessary, which can have the perverse effect of creating a targeted group that is in fact less qualified, reinforcing negative stereotypes. Of course, discrimination might also discourage education or effort, if those discriminated against fear that they will not be appropriately rewarded in the marketplace. In practice, women and minorities have long undertaken substantial investments in education and increased their commitment to the labor market, even when discrimination was far more overt and significant than today.

Affirmative action can even be counterproductive if affected firms seek to avoid legal punishment by not hiring the targeted group in the first place. If a firm employs no women, for example, it cannot be sued for paying its female employees less than its male employees or for failing to promote women in sufficient numbers. If a firm employs no disabled persons, it cannot be sued for failing to provide "reasonable accommodations."

At a more mundane level, affirmative action generates compliance costs because firms must document the relevant aspects of their hiring, credit, or admissions policies and incur legal costs related to affirmative action lawsuits.

Whatever the magnitude of affirmative action's costs, a crucial question is whether affirmative action has reduced discrimination. The evidence shows only a modest effect in narrowing wage gaps or improving credit access for minorities or women. These gaps have generally diminished over time, but much of the narrowing predates implementation of affirmative action—which means forces other than affirmative action, such as increased education for blacks and women, have played a bigger role in reducing race and gender differentials.

The view that governments should not mandate affirmative action is distinct from any assessment of private, voluntary affirmative action. Many examples of such behavior exist, such as private colleges and universities that practice affirmative action in admissions. Private reverse discrimination should be entirely legal, and the fact that many private entities find it in their interests to practice affirmative action is one reason that government affirmative action is not necessary.

agricultural subsidies

Most economies subsidize the production of agricultural products, whether via price supports, payments for crops not grown, government-funded research on fertilizers, or reduced-price water supplies. The amounts of taxpayer largesse are substantial in many economies.

Elimination of agricultural subsidies is an elemental no-brainer in the economic policy world. These subsidies transfer large sums from the taxpayer to farmers, especially high-income farmers. By reducing food production, moreover, the subsidies raise food prices, which harms everyone. By encouraging food production in places where it is not economically efficient, subsidies also distort society's allocation of resources.

The persistence of agricultural subsidies is a useful test case for the ability of economic arguments to shape policy (free **trade** is another good example). Despite near consensus among economists that subsidies make no sense on either efficiency or distributional grounds, they persist.

The most plausible explanation is that the winners (rich farmers) constitute a small, concentrated group that has the incentive and ability to lobby for its preferred policy. The losers (everyone who eats) constitute a large, diverse group, and no one person suffers that much. If, say, the United States spends $15 billion per year on subsidies and has over 300 million people, food costs are higher by less than $50 per person. This provides little incentive for any individual to organize a political action committee (PAC) or set up a lobbying organization to oppose agricultural subsidies.

anti-poverty programs

Modern societies take as given that governments should help the poor. Consistent with this view, governments provide cash, food, housing, medical care, education, and more to low-income households.

The standard argument for anti-poverty programs holds that differences in income result significantly from luck—low IQ, the "wrong" skin color, lousy parents, and so on—rather than from effort. Thus, many argue, governments should redistribute to the poor out of compassion or fairness. Alternatively, some suggest that, if asked before knowing whether they would be rich or poor (behind a so-called veil of ignorance about their economic future), most people would voluntarily pay to make sure they did not end up in poverty. So, governments should provide anti-poverty spending as a kind of social insurance.

This perspective on poverty has some merit. Inherited differences in health, skill, intelligence, wealth, nationality, skin color, and sex, along with random events, undoubtedly explain some income differences, especially those between the very poor and everyone else. Private charity cares for some of those who suffer bad luck, but private actions might be inadequate if some people do not contribute and instead assume the charity provided by others is sufficient (the "free-rider" problem).

Anti-poverty programs are nevertheless problematic.

Private efforts to alleviate poverty are substantial. Religious institutions operate soup kitchens, the Boy Scouts organize food drives, the Salvation Army raises money for the poor, Habitat for Humanity builds houses, and Doctors Without Borders provides health care. Families care for many of the poor, and immigrants send remittances to relatives left behind. Many at risk of poverty can accumulate personal savings or obtain loans and gifts from family and friends. Thus the view that markets will not care for the poor is, at a minimum, exaggerated. Relatedly, the amount of private charity appears to decline as the amount of government charity increases, so public efforts seem to crowd out private giving.

Private anti-poverty measures may still be insufficient, but their deficiencies must be balanced against the fact that government anti-poverty programs have substantial costs.

Anti-poverty programs distort the incentives to work and save. Whether these effects are large depends on the generosity of the programs: a promise of subsistence income will induce only a few people to live off assistance, while a more substantial guarantee will cause many to reduce their effort. The level of anti-poverty spending is generous in developed economies. Low-income households are eligible for cash grants, subsidized medical care, public schooling, energy assistance, and reduced-price housing. The implied equivalent income dwarfs average income in developing economies and middle-class income from a few decades ago in developed economies. It follows, then, that this generosity reduces effort.

These programs also affect society generally. Anti-poverty programs generate envy and therefore stimulate the near poor to demand transfers, which in turn encourages redistribution beyond alleviation of poverty, with larger efficiency losses. Anti-poverty programs promote the view that low income is someone else's fault. This is often true, but enshrining this outlook in policy is likely to reduce society's work ethic. This harms everyone because members of society then devote their energy to chasing transfers rather than to innovation and productivity.

Whatever the ex-ante merits of anti-poverty programs, and however large their unintended consequences, anti-poverty programs have not obviously reduced poverty. Although spending on such programs has grown enormously in the United States and other countries, poverty rates have not necessarily fallen and in some cases have increased. Foreign aid aimed at Third World poverty has had minimal impact.

A separate question from *whether* to have anti-poverty programs is *what kind* we might want. The libertarian view is that a **negative income tax** is the best approach, and that all anti-poverty programs should be left to state rather than federal governments (see **federalism**).

See also **flat tax, redistributing income, utilitarianism.**

antitrust policy

One way governments attempt to promote a productive economy is by outlawing monopoly and related business practices, such as agreements among competitors to raise prices. These and other antitrust policies might seem beneficial given the conclusion from economics that competition enhances economic efficiency. Competition is indeed good, but antitrust has significant costs and can diminish rather than enhance competition.

The first reason for caution is that market power—the ability of a business to charge excessive prices—appears to be modest in most industries. When the firms in an industry earn monopoly profits, it encourages new firms to enter and compete for these profits until all firms earn a normal rate of return. In particular, excess profits invite imitation and innovation, which erodes market power over time. Even explicit agreements between competitors to raise prices rarely last because the participants often cheat by producing more output than the agreement stipulates.

Thus the problem for which antitrust is allegedly the solution is not necessarily large in the first place. Moreover, antitrust has negative side effects.

The main component of antitrust policy is restrictions on mergers that would give the consolidated firm "too large" a share of industry sales. The downside is that antitrust also prevents mergers that would improve economic efficiency. Bigger firms produce more efficiently than smaller firms, and many mergers are attempts to reap the benefits of increased size. Antitrust also reduces the threat of takeover faced by incompetent managers, thus allowing inept or corrupt firms to persist. Antitrust gives weak firms a new strategy: They can complain to antitrust authorities about allegedly anti-competitive behavior by their competitors, rather than improving their own products or cutting costs. Antitrust generates uncertainty and delay as firms ponder the response of antitrust authorities to proposed mergers.

Perhaps most important, antitrust diminishes the incentive to innovate, precisely because it limits monopoly profits. These profits signal entrepreneurs and inventors that a profit opportunity exists from creating products that compete with the monopolist. The explosion of personal computer manufacturers, which did far more than antitrust to eliminate IBM's dominant position, is a textbook example. A modest level of monopoly profits in the short run is a small price to pay for increased productivity over the long run.

See also **professional licensure.**

arbitrary redistributions

A common adverse effect of government policies is redistributions of income that make no sense from either an efficiency or distributional perspective. **Agricultural subsidies** seek to help farmers, but this is not a sensible goal since most farmers are not poor. Tariffs, quotas, and other trade restrictions aim to protect certain industries, but this is bad economics since market forces rather than political connections should determine which industries survive and which fail. Once government is in the business of handing out special favors, moreover, businesses engage in unproductive efforts to win these pots of money and to promote creation of these windfalls.

Government also causes arbitrary redistribution even when policy has defensible objectives. Consider government construction projects, whether for housing, schools, roads, or hospitals. Governments typically hire private contractors for this work, and in principle the governments can simply auction off these contracts to the lowest bidder. In practice identifying the right firm to undertake a specific project, and getting it done at an appropriate price, is difficult. Governments often pay more than costs plus a fair return to ensure someone bids on the contract. Governments have difficulty monitoring progress and quality, so they often get less than they contracted for. Thus the companies lucky enough to get these contracts—and not necessarily the deserving ones—get rich at the expense of taxpayers.

The fact that some firms benefit from government projects does not by itself make interventions undesirable. But giving interest groups an incentive to encourage creation of these pockets of money is a major cost. Construction companies and construction unions, for example, are likely to argue for building more highways and undertaking more maintenance than an unbiased evaluation would support.

The arbitrary redistributions caused by government can sometimes be reduced or eliminated using a smaller-government approach, in those cases where intervention does occur. Subsidizing education or housing through vouchers, for example, means that government does not need to construct school buildings or housing projects.

arts and culture

Governments subsidize arts and culture in a number of ways: by making grants to individual artists, by owning and operating museums, by funding performing arts organizations like symphony orchestras, and even by running **zoos**. The claim made for these subsidies is that art and culture are vital parts of a nation's social or historical fabric, but that private markets will undersupply such activities because no one takes account of the beneficial effects on society from maintaining art and culture.

Without governmental intervention, some artistic or cultural activities might not survive on their own in the marketplace, but that just means market demand is insufficient. The claim that these activities generate beneficial spillovers is difficult to confirm or quantify, and it begs the question of who gets to decide what is worth subsidizing and what is not. Thus government funding for arts and culture is in practice just a handout to elites under the guise of benevolence.

See also **sports stadiums.**

asymmetric information and adverse selection

One common justification for a number of government policies, including insurance regulation, credit subsidies, and consumer protection regulation, is that, in certain settings, participants on opposite sides of the market have asymmetric information about factors that are relevant to a transaction between them. A health insurance company does not necessarily know whether applicants for insurance engage in a healthy lifestyle; if it did, the company would charge a higher premium to those with poor eating or exercise habits. A bank does not necessarily know which loan applicants are innately honest and will diligently try to repay; if it did, the bank would offer a lower interest rate to such applicants.

When this kind of asymmetry of information exists, the presumption that private markets are efficient breaks down. Consider the health insurance market as illustration.

If health insurers cannot tell who is likely to remain healthy and who is not, they must charge everyone the same premium. If this premium reflects the average health of the population, only unhealthy persons find the insurance worth purchasing. In economics lingo, the insurer ends up with an adverse selection of insurees, so the insurance company goes broke. Recognizing this, insurers exit the market or charge a premium consistent with the average health expenditure of unhealthy consumers, and healthy consumers do not want to purchase this insurance. Healthy consumers can still purchase health care on a fee-for-service basis, but these consumers face expenditures that vary unpredictably over time rather paying regular insurance premiums.

This is where advocates point to government intervention. Government could mandate that everyone purchase insurance at a price that just allows insurance companies to make a fair rate of profit on average. Then, the insurance program balances financially, and everyone gets insurance at the actuarially fair price.

The asymmetric information hypothesis is an intellectually coherent defense of health insurance mandates. Whether it is a convincing justification in practice is a different question. The key issue is that insurance companies may be able to reduce the information asymmetry substantially—for instance, by requiring medical exams and thus obtaining much of the health information known to the applicant. Other cases of asymmetric information allow similar private fixes.

Thus the assumption underlying the adverse selection story does not apply in all instances where it has been employed as a justification for government policies. The case for these interventions is therefore weaker than usually asserted.

See also **consumer protection, health insurance, subsidizing education.**

bank regulation and deposit insurance

Regulation of banking is pervasive in modern economies. Banks must purchase government deposit insurance, and banks face rules about what kinds of assets they can hold and how much risk they can take on in their investments.

The justification for this kind of regulation is that unregulated banks might be subject to frequent bank runs and panics because banks lend out most of their deposits and hold only a fraction as cash. A widespread demand for withdrawals, perhaps caused by a loan default or corruption scandal, can therefore cause the affected bank to fail. Worse, a run on one bank can increase depositor concerns at other banks, leading to contagion and financial panic.

Deposit insurance eliminates the incentive for bank runs by promising depositors they will receive all their money even if the bank fails. This means depositors have no reason to run on a bank in the first place.

The problem with deposit insurance is that it generates a **moral hazard**; when banks know their deposits are insured, they have an incentive to purchase riskier assets. If these assets generate high returns, banks make good profits, while if they fail, deposit insurance cushions the blow. Thus banks assume more risk than warranted by market fundamentals.

To alleviate the moral hazard created by deposit insurance, regulation limits bank holdings of risky assets and requires a minimum degree of capitalization. In principle this "balance-sheet" regulation can counter deposit insurance's tendency to generate excessive risk taking, but in practice banks can innovate around the regulation. Thus, they can still end up taking more risk than is appropriate.

This is precisely what occurred in the run-up to the Financial Crisis of 2008. By using derivatives, off-balance-sheet vehicles, and "structured finance," banks were able to assume huge risks within the confines of existing regulation. For several years the excessive risk taking generated large profits, but eventually the underlying fundamentals crashed, pushing several large banks to the brink of failure. Widespread failure did not occur because of a Treasury bailout, but the adverse implications for taxpayers were plausibly at least as bad as those that failure would have imposed (see **too big to fail**).

Any regulatory attempt to limit moral hazard faces similar problems. Balance sheet regulation can fail because banks innovate around it or move their activities offshore to less regulated institutions. Balance sheet regulation can also fail because regulators do not have the will to close irresponsible banks or because of incompetence or corruption at the regulatory agencies. So long as the incentive exists for banks to off-load risk onto government deposit insurance, regulatory control is likely to be ineffective.

In contrast, the incentive for bank runs and panics can be vastly reduced by eliminating an existing regulation, the ban on suspension of convertibility. This aspect of regulation says that when depositors request cash withdrawals, banks must comply. Absent this regulation, banks might offer deposit contracts that allowed partial or full suspension during panics of the right to convert deposits into cash. These contracts would presumably differ in additional ways from standard demand deposits. For example, they might require interest on suspended balances or specify how long a bank could suspend without a penalty. They would not, however, commit the bank to meeting all deposit withdrawals immediately.

If banks can suspend convertibility, depositors know that runs merely precipitate suspension, greatly reducing depositor incentive to panic and run. Allowing banks to suspend would probably not eliminate all runs, but it would plausibly limit them to banks that are insolvent rather than merely illiquid. Deposit insurance and balance sheet regulation become irrelevant.

Before 1914, by law U.S. banks could not suspend, but many did so anyway, sometimes with explicit approval of, or encouragement from, regulators. This did not eliminate runs and panics, but suspension did reduce contagion and failure. A few panics were associated with substantial declines in output, but many were short term and geographically confined. When recession and panic overlapped, the line of causation often ran from recession to bank solvency, rather than from panics to recessions. Suspension would be even more effective if banks were able to experiment with different contracts and suspend without fear of legal jeopardy.

The socially desirable number of runs, moreover, is not zero. After all, runs discipline banks that take excessive risks. In an idealized setting the mere threat of runs might be sufficient to make banks behave prudently, but in the real world the occasional run is necessary to close down irresponsible or incompetent banks and to remind others to behave.

Both theory and evidence, therefore, suggest that an unregulated banking system would perform as well or better than a system of deposit insurance combined with balance sheet regulation.

bans on discrimination

Some people make decisions on the basis of factors such as race or sex, and such actions are widely viewed as unfair. Many countries, therefore, ban discrimination in employment, housing, lending, admissions, and other areas. These bans typically apply to discrimination based on race, sex, religious preference, sexual orientation, and other characteristics. The magnitude of **discrimination** in market economies is not necessarily large, but even if it is substantial, bans can do more harm than good.

Policy cannot target discrimination without limiting how private parties can use their own property. That is, bans adopt the view that businesses and other private institutions are partially public and can therefore be told to operate in socially approved ways. Blurring the distinction between private and public, however, legitimizes government interventions that are unnecessary or even counterproductive. In the discrimination context, the notion that a business is partly public might be used to ban private affirmative action if this is regarded as impermissible (reverse) discrimination.

Beyond this problem, bans on discrimination provide only a weak check on discrimination. Any decision to hire, promote, or admit reflects numerous considerations, and judges and juries can rarely know the true motives of an alleged discriminator. Thus policy cannot in practice ban discrimination while avoiding **affirmative action**, as U.S. experience illustrates. The original defense of the **Civil Rights Act of 1964**, the U.S. law that outlawed discrimination in hiring, argued that it contained no language mandating quotas. Within a few years, however, the act was used to impose quotas widely.

The question for policy, therefore, is not whether bans on discrimination are desirable but whether bans plus affirmative action are beneficial overall. The libertarian answer is no.

See also **affirmative action**.

budget deficits

A budget deficit occurs when the government spends more than it collects in tax revenue. Government borrows the difference and repays it later using future tax revenues.

One aspect of budget deficits is their role in **stabilization policies**. An increase in the deficit might provide a **fiscal stimulus** that reduces or averts a recession, so policy makers in modern economies often attempt to adjust the deficit in the short-run to smooth out the business cycle.

A different aspect of budget deficits is their implication for the size of government. In fact, the deficit is a terrible measure of government's influence. The deficit is the difference between two quantities—revenues and taxes—so any given deficit is consistent with big government (high expenditure, high taxes) or small government (low expenditure, low taxes).

The crucial question in the long run, therefore, is how government spends the money it raises in taxes, not whether it pays for this spending with taxes raised now or taxes raised later. If government spends its revenue on productive activities that the private sector does not undertake, then this spending makes sense whether the current deficit is large or small. Otherwise, the spending is bad policy, regardless of the deficit.

campaign finance regulation

Most governments limit political contributions and restrict campaign spending by politicians and parties. This campaign finance regulation also limits political communications, such as issue ads.

The argument for campaign finance regulation rests on four claims: that spending by politicians affects their likelihood of election; that contributions to political campaigns affect the policies a politician supports; that these influences on political outcomes are undesirable; and that regulation successfully limits money's influence on these outcomes. Each of these claims is problematic.

Neither theory nor evidence indicates that spending has a large impact on a candidate's electoral success. Low-spending candidates can obtain free publicity by generating newsworthy quotes or via campaign appearances at opportune times and locations. The quality of a candidate's message, rather than the mere quantity, plays an important role in electability, and candidates attract money because they have a popular message. Thus spending is only one part of winning elections.

Contributions are not determinative regarding policy positions because democracies count votes, not dollars, and the non-rich outnumber the rich. Thus politicians cannot accommodate contributors whose interests are out of step with substantial voting blocs. In fact, most economies have numerous policies that money presumably opposes: progressive income taxation, **union** protections, **environmental policies,** occupational safety and health regulation, zoning laws, expanded voting rights, and more. Groups with both the votes and the money, moreover, have voted against narrow self-interest, such as men giving women the right to vote.

Whether spending affects elections or contributions affect candidate positions, money's influence is not necessarily bad. Money lines up behind certain issues because a larger economic pie coincides with that perspective. Some environmentalists oppose cost-benefit analysis, for example, because this might not favor the policies they prefer. From an efficiency perspective, however, it is good that businesses or consumers bring economic impacts into the discussion. Special interests do support bad policies, including corporate welfare, tariffs and quotas, **agricultural subsidies**, wasteful weapons programs, and pork-barrel spending, but this is only one side of the ledger.

Even if money's influence is deleterious on net, regulation is unlikely to reduce that influence. Under full public funding, for example, independent groups could still spend money that purports to address a specific policy but implicitly supports a candidate. Under this regime, politicians could still adjust their positions to secure donations. Lawmakers could regulate these issue ads, but this would be a blatant stifling of free speech. Such regulation would be ineffective in any case because politicians can communicate via the Internet and other means.

The standard arguments for campaign finance regulation are thus not persuasive, and regulation has deleterious consequences.

Regulation raises the costs of becoming a politician or organizing a political party, which stifles political competition. Regulation rewards dishonest politicians and parties because it allows multiple avenues for creative interpretation (see **disrespect for the law**).

Regulation lulls voters and the media into thinking that government has solved the problem of interest-group politics, but since money will always find a way to exercise its influence, this is a false sense of security.

Regulation is **thought control** because taking a stance against money in politics is not a neutral position. Rather, the anti-money position lines up with particular views about how the economy operates, about which policies are beneficial, and so on. Limiting money's influence is thus an attempt to limit ideas, thought, and speech—while trying to convince the public that it is not.

Although government mechanisms for disciplining politicians do not work, private mechanisms would perform reasonably if government attempts stopped. The media would produce stories about candidates' receipt of contributions or their refusal to disclose their sources, and the Internet would disseminate this information almost instantly. Independent groups like the League of Women Voters or Common Cause would ask politicians to disclose their sources of funds and make this information available to voters. These groups and the media would also reveal lying by politicians.

capital punishment

Many governments have imposed the death penalty for serious crimes such as homicide. Most countries abandoned the death penalty during the 20th century, but a few, such as China, Iran, Saudi Arabia, North Korea, and Pakistan, still employ it with some frequency. The practice is relatively rare but nevertheless contentious in the United States.

Death penalty supporters rely on three arguments. First, that the possibility of capital punishment deters crime by increasing the expected punishment that confronts rational, forward-looking murderers. Second, that executing criminals convicted of the most serious crimes is cheaper than incarcerating them for life. Third, that murderers deserve to die.

None of these arguments is persuasive. Decades of social science research finds little evidence that the death penalty deters murder. Some murderers are not forward-looking (e.g., perpetrators of crimes of passion), and forward-looking murderers correctly believe their chances of being executed, even if arrested and convicted, are low and will only occur years or decades after conviction. The monetary savings from use of the death penalty are overstated, since fighting appeals from death row prisoners is costly. Moral considerations do not resolve the issue because many people believe it is wrong for the state to take a life, no matter how heinous the crime.

The death penalty, moreover, has unintended consequences. Capital punishment eliminates the possibility of correcting mistakes. This is not an enormous effect if most convicted murderers are guilty, but everyone benefits from correcting the mistakes that do occur. As with **gun control**, the death penalty is a distraction. Society wastes substantial energy arguing about the death penalty rather than focusing on policies that would actually reduce crime, such as ending **drug prohibition**, legalizing **prostitution**, and improving educational outcomes.

central banks and monetary policy

A central bank is a government-chartered financial institution that controls the stock of money and interest rates, facilitates check clearing around the country, and supervises the regulation of private banks. Its most important activity is adjusting the money stock and interest rates to reduce the magnitude of business cycles and promote economic growth.

Whether central banks improve economic performance is part of the broader question of whether **stabilization policies** help more often than they hurt. The libertarian assessment is that stabilization, while defensible in principle, is difficult in practice and probably increases rather than decreases volatility on net. It follows that central banks are unnecessary or even counterproductive, since the non-stabilization activities of central banks can be addressed by other regulators, or by the private sector (e.g., check clearing). The only government intervention that is needed regarding money is establishing what form of payment the government accepts for those transactions it must conduct. This may in practice establish a default money, but private forces can do everything else related to money, such as developing alternative means of payment like credit or debit cards.

The notion that economies do not need central banks might seem radical, but the United States did not have a central bank until 1914, and many other countries adopted them only late in the 19th century. Likewise, states do not have central banks, and many countries have pegged their currency to that of another country, such as the U.S. dollar, thus ceding control of their monetary policy. These economies without central banks have, overall, developed and progressed as much as those with central banks.

children

Governments pursue numerous policies that aim to protect children, including compulsory education laws, bans on child labor, adoption laws, mandatory child car seats, warning labels on toys, and required vaccinations. Some children suffer serious harm due to bad parental decisions, and laws designed to protect children have good intentions. **Paternalism** toward children is more defensible than paternalism toward adults, moreover, because the presumption of rational decision making is less compelling. Thus laws to protect children can make sense, but caution is nevertheless in order.

Parents can (and do) mess up their children in myriad ways, so attempts to improve one parental choice can worsen another or get lost in a sea of mistakes. Compulsory education laws, for example, might reduce parents' incentive to think about whether school is a good use of their children's time. Even when the right choice is similar for most parents, exceptions exist, so policies that impose one approach on all children and parents have costs. Most children benefit from being in school through a certain age, for example, but for some an apprenticeship at age 14 would make more sense. Further, intervening in parental choice, in anything other than the most extreme situations, starts policy down a **slippery slope**.

Policies that aim to keep children safe or healthy are the ones most likely to generate more benefits than costs: mandating that infants ride in car seats, or requiring vaccinations against infectious diseases for young children, are reasonable examples. Even these policies deserve careful scrutiny, however. Some parents ignore the mandates on car seats, or install them incorrectly, and these seats are expensive, so the net benefit is not necessarily large. Most parents would get their children vaccinated without a requirement, so again the net benefit of this policy may be minimal.

The bottom line is not that all child-protection policies are bad but that policy should restrict itself to the most egregious parental abuses or attempt gentle nudges rather than hard shoves. For example, child labor laws should differ across countries in line with level of economic development. Imposing a minimum work age of 14 in a rich country does little harm; kids up to this age have reasonable opportunities for education, their families rarely need the income support, and most jobs require more skill than such children possess anyway. In developing countries these conditions do not hold, so minimum work ages should be lower or absent. Requiring that children be in some kind of seat belt or restraint may make sense; insisting on state-of-the-art car seats probably does not. Providing free but voluntary vaccinations to children in low-income families is less coercive than a universal requirement and targeted at those least likely to get vaccinations on their own.

Civil Rights Act of 1964

Advocates of bans on discrimination typically point to Title VII of the Civil Rights Act of 1964, which banned employment discrimination in the United States, as evidence that bans are crucial for ending discrimination. Essentially the argument is that the employment and wage outcomes of blacks relative to whites improved in the U.S. South in the decade after 1964, and this outcome is most readily explained as the result of Title VII.

The role played by Title VII in improving economic outcomes for blacks is far from clear, however. To begin, adoption and enforcement of Title VII occurred against a backdrop of legally enforced segregation in southern states, segregation that applied in education, public accommodations, and voting (the Jim Crow laws). Some of the improved outcomes for blacks undoubtedly reflect the toppling of this legal structure, which had facilitated the culture of discrimination even in arenas, like employment, where segregation was rarely legally mandated.

Adding further nuance, private efforts to end segregation, including boycotts and protests, occurred before and after passage of the Civil Rights Act. Likewise, the federal government intervened to end segregation even before 1964. For example, the Supreme Court's *Brown v. Board of Education* decision began the process of integrating public schools, and federal court orders repealed state segregation in transportation. Thus the degree to which Title VII itself caused the improved outcomes for blacks is unclear.

Whatever the role of Title VII in generating gains for blacks, it is not the whole story. These gains would likely have come anyway—perhaps somewhat more slowly—due to private efforts and the federal dismantling of Jim Crow. In addition, the act's ban on discrimination led to further interventions that have generated far more costs and produced far less evidence for their efficacy. In particular, the Civil Rights Act evolved into **affirmative action**, and the scope of anti-discrimination policy evolved from merely outlawing racism to promoting diversity and limiting statistical discrimination.

Thus, the federal effort to eliminate discriminatory state laws was almost certainly desirable, but the efforts beyond this intervention have probably not been beneficial overall.

consequential versus philosophical libertarianism

Libertarianism comes in two flavors: consequential and philosophical (also known as rights-based). The two variants offer similar policy conclusions but utilize seemingly different arguments to arrive at these conclusions.

Consequentialism—the path followed in this book—argues that most government interventions are undesirable because they fail to achieve their stated goals or because they generate costs that are worse than the problems they purport to fix. In particular, consequentialism emphasizes that many policies have **unintended consequences**. The consequentialist approach is thus just a **cost-benefit** calculation, albeit one with a broad view of costs and benefits. In particular, the consequentialist approach recognizes that policies have intangible and non-monetary effects, not just tangible or monetary effects.

Philosophical libertarians hold that government should never infringe individual rights or freedoms. Key among these rights are ownership of one's person and property. Philosophical libertarians therefore oppose all government policies except those that protect individuals against infringement of their rights. Philosophical libertarians accept a role for government in defending the country and in defining and enforcing property rights, but in no other arena.

At first blush, the consequential and philosophical perspectives might seem to be radically different approaches to evaluating policies. Yet this difference is more apparent than real.

Philosophical libertarianism is in fact a consequentialist perspective; it has simply concluded that principles like "always respect individual rights" are useful rules-of-thumb for balancing the positive and negative consequences of intervention. When interventions infringe individual rights to a non-trivial degree, a broad range of negatives follow and outweigh any benefits from intervention. Thus, it is reasonable to assume that policies that infringe rights are bad policies.

Stated differently, the philosophical libertarian assertion that policy should protect individual rights is really a statement that adhering to this principle promotes human happiness, or social progress, or something. Respecting this principle, argue philosophical libertarians, has good consequences. In this sense, the philosophical libertarian principle is no different than other values or principles such as morality or justice, which, properly interpreted, are also rules-of-thumb based on assessments of underlying consequences.

The two versions of libertarianism are thus not fundamentally different, even though they appear so to some observers. The explicitly consequentialist approach is nevertheless a better language than the rights-based approach for explaining libertarianism.

To begin, philosophically based defenses of libertarian policy conclusions seem to be assertions that lack factual justification. In particular, the assertion that policy should never infringe individual rights is just that—an assertion. Libertarians think this is a good rule of thumb for designing government, but many non-libertarians advocate some different guidepost, such as equalizing the distribution of income. Arguments over which principle is better are rarely productive because they leave discussion of consequences in the background, and most people care ultimately about the consequences of polices. Thus many people accept the consequentialist approach once it is made explicit, and this increases the scope for productive discussion.

Being explicitly consequentialist is more readily consistent with the view that among undesirable policies, some are much worse than others, a point that can get lost in the absolutist-sounding language of philosophical libertarianism. A policy that generates many serious consequences and few sizable benefits is worse than one that generates only small adverse effects and moderate benefits. Similarly, some policy approaches are worse than others, even if both infringe individual rights. The consequentialist ability to reach nuanced conclusions makes it more broadly acceptable than philosophical libertarianism. Even people who are skeptical of big government find it implausible that every government policy is equally bad, so they sometimes dismiss philosophical libertarianism as too narrow or rigid.

A related benefit of being explicitly consequentialist is that it permits reasoned compromise. The philosophical approach makes this more difficult by appearing to insist that all interventions are utterly unacceptable. Philosophical libertarians, for example, sometimes describe income redistribution as theft, which makes it hard to compromise with people who believe otherwise. The consequential perspective notes the unintended but negative consequences of redistribution, such as discouraging productive activity, but it does not rule out redistribution a priori. Thus consequentialists can potentially convince egalitarians that too much redistribution is undesirable, whether or not one believes in redistribution as a matter of principle.

The consequential approach also avoids the logical difficulties fostered by the language of the philosophical perspective. Philosophical libertarians accept that government should defend the country from attack, but this position is silent on the appropriate size of the military. Should an army consist of one soldier? Ten thousand? One million? As soon as one says "big enough to defend the country," one has made a consequentialist argument, accepting that a tradeoff exists between costs and benefits in determining the right policy.

Similarly, if government exists at all, it must levy taxes to pay for its expenditures, yet the philosophical approach seems to suggest that all taxation is illegitimate. The consequential approach recognizes explicitly that government expenditure can be beneficial (e.g., for national defense), so some taxation is a necessary evil. The balancing involved in consequentialism is more difficult than simply asserting principles, but it provides a logical and consistent way to assess the appropriate role for government, however small. Philosophical discussions provide little basis for analyzing these kinds of trade-offs.

People who want to emphasize liberty, of course, are free to include it as a consequence of limited government. The explicitly consequentialist approach simply forces such arguments to discuss the possible trade-offs between liberty and other effects of policy.

conservatism versus libertarianism

The principles that underlie the conservative view are not obvious, at least not in the contemporary political landscape. Proponents of conservatism often claim a "small government" perspective, yet conservatism advocates big government in many areas, including foreign policy interventions and drug prohibition. Further, conservative politicians have endorsed a wide range of interventionist government when it seemed politically expedient to do so (e.g., the George W. Bush administration's support for No Child Left Behind, **campaign finance regulation**, and the Medicare prescription drug benefit).

Conservatism and libertarianism are thus radically different in practice even though popular discussion sometimes lumps them together. Roughly, conservatism and libertarianism tend to overlap regarding economic issues but not on social or foreign policy issues. As illustration, consider conservatism's and libertarianism's positions on alcohol and marijuana. Conservatives want to prohibit marijuana but not alcohol even though any objective accounting suggests alcohol is the more dangerous substance. Libertarians want both goods to be legal, not because either is benign but because the consequences of prohibition are worse than the consequences of legal availability of either good.

Conservatism pays lip service to numerous underlying principles, from the value of private enterprise, to the virtues of small government, to respecting states rights. Conservatism is nevertheless inconsistent in these and other dimensions. To give one example, conservatives oppose states' rights when it comes to medical marijuana but support such rights when it comes to abortion.

More broadly, the conservative desire for government intervention regarding a broad range of social issues suggests that conservatives do not believe people can make good choices on their own and that government should intervene to improve those choices. Thus conservatism is at its essence a **paternalistic** position that assumes government knows better than the people being governed.

consumer protection

Numerous government policies aim to outlaw or regulate businesses' tactics that might deceive or harm consumers. These policies include bans on **false or misleading advertising**, bans on products or features deemed excessively dangerous (e.g., cars without seatbelts), lemon laws (which give consumers the right to return used cars that have defects), usury laws (which set maximum interest rates), anti-scalping laws (which prevent resale of tickets to concerts or sporting events), and required warning labels on toys or nutritional labels on processed foods.

The standard justification holds that consumers are naïve about the claims businesses make for their products and are therefore easily swayed to purchase products they do not need or that do not deliver as promised. At the same time, the standard justification asserts that businesses focus mainly on short-run profits and therefore use shady tactics for immediate gain rather then developing good customer relations and a reputation for quality products.

No one doubts that some businesses prey on unsophisticated consumers, but policies that aim to protect consumers are problematic.

Consumer protection policies raise the costs of doing business, so the affected products are more expensive. Required ingredient labels on food or warning labels on toys, for example, constitute an additional expense for the companies that make these products. Sometimes these costs are relatively trivial for large firms but more significant for small firms, so the requirements put the latter at a disadvantage and reduce competition and increase prices even more than implied by the added costs themselves.

Consumer protection policies also enshrine the view that consumers are too stupid to think for themselves. By adopting this stance, policy may convince consumers that government has addressed the problem of business misconduct and discourage consumers from engaging in their own due diligence. Government cannot identify every misleading business tactic or intervene in every instance, however, so consumers will end up being misled at times unless they use their own brains.

A more effective check on disreputable business practices is competition between businesses. When firms engage in tactics that mislead consumers, rival firms have ample incentive to rebut those claims (so long as laws against **false or misleading advertising** are not too strict). Relatedly, consumers reward firms that engage in honest business practices by giving them repeat business. Fair dealing over the long run also tends to make consumers wary of fly-by-night shops that might be more likely to rip them off.

A different mechanism for holding businesses accountable is **product liability**. Under these laws, consumers who are injured by faulty products or do not get what they were promised can sue businesses for damages. These claims against businesses originate with actions by consumers, but government serves as referee by trying the lawsuits and enforcing the decisions. This disciplines firms that misbehave while imposing only small costs on responsible businesses.

consumption taxes

The main tax system in most developed economies employs income as the tax base; the taxes owed depend on the amount of wage, salary, interest, dividend, capital gains, and other income earned. An alternative is to use consumption as the tax base. Under this approach, taxpayers who earn the same amount of income but consume different proportions pay different amounts of tax. Quite simply, you are taxed on what you spend rather than what you earn. The greater the amount consumed (the less saved), the higher is the amount of taxes. In the consumption tax system typically proposed, the same tax rate applies to every dollar of consumption, whether it's your first or your last.

The advantage of consumption taxation is that it promotes saving (and therefore capital accumulation) relative to income taxation. Higher saving means greater investment, which enhances economic productivity because the labor force gets more machinery and equipment to produce goods and services, as well as more research and development.

Some object to consumption taxation because it falls more heavily on the poor than does income taxation. Low-income households spend most of their income rather than saving it, so under a (flat) consumption tax they face higher tax rates (relative to income) than middle- and upper-income households.

A possible response is to make the tax rates on consumption increase with the amount of income (that is, make them progressive rather than proportional). While feasible, such a modification loses the simplicity, administrative convenience, and efficiency of a flat rate.

A consumption tax with progressive rates is perhaps still a reasonable compromise; whether it differs substantially from income taxation depends on the overall amount of taxation. If the level of government expenditure, and thus taxation, were at the level libertarians advocate, the efficiency benefits of consumption as opposed to income taxation would be small.

corporate income tax

Many countries tax the income earned by corporations, which serves as double taxation of corporate income because personal tax systems normally cover both dividends and capital gains. The usual justification for this double taxation is that it makes high-income taxpayers—the corporation owners—pay their fair share.

While some of the tax's impact falls on owners—it reduces after-tax profits and therefore the dividends and capital gains that shareholders receive—owners are more than happy to pass on their additional costs to others. Much of the impact falls on the corporation's employees, who take a hit in the form of lower wages, and on the corporation's customers, who face the higher prices a corporation charges when its costs increase. High taxation can also push corporations overseas, reducing employment and further harming employees. In other words, the tax burden falls on all of us.

Corporate income taxation has other significant negatives. It reduces the incentive to save because it lowers the dividends and capital gains earned from owning shares of corporations. Reduced saving means lower capital accumulation and economic growth, which hurts everyone, rich and poor, stakeholders and others.

Corporate income taxation also requires rules and regulations over and above the personal income tax system, which is itself immensely complex. This not only creates significant compliance costs but also favors specific industries or kinds of projects, thus distorting private investment decisions and creating the incentive to game the government rather than just investing in industries that seem profitable. Corporate income taxation reduces the transparency of corporate accounting, making it harder for investors to monitor corporate behavior.

Governments that tax corporate income have also seen fit to exempt certain activities from corporate taxation by designating them as nonprofits. The fundamental assumption here is that some activities—especially those provided by schools, churches, arts organizations, and charities—are socially beneficial. This assumption may be true, but it allows government to decide what constitutes education, religion, art, or charity, to the exclusion of other groups that fulfill the same purpose. The decisions inevitably favor the status quo and suppress competition. For example, the IRS might not award nonprofit status to a chain of vocational tech schools for teenagers, even though public schools and private for-profits often provide the same instruction.

The corporate tax system also has the odd effect of making it seem that inanimate objects pay taxes. Only people pay taxes—something everyone needs to understand lest they think government can raise taxes without distorting economic decisions or affecting individuals. Every decision to tax affects real people and impacts far more than the direct target of the tax.

corruption

Bribes, kickbacks, and other payments made to evade a law or regulation are present in every society and widespread in many. Politicians and the media bemoan this corruption and often pass laws designed to curtail it. This response does nothing to reduce corruption and often makes it worse.

Corruption arises mainly because of laws that impede private profit opportunities or interfere with mutually beneficial exchange. If government requires a fee or license to operate a certain kind of business or enter a particular profession, then people who are so interested might find it cheaper to bribe the relevant official than to pay for the license or permit. That's especially true if the likelihood of being caught is low, or if the fine for the bribery is lower than the possible gains. If policy tries to outlaw vice transactions like drug sales or prostitution, the affected parties have an incentive to bribe the police to avoid arrest. If the government awards large sums to private contractors for building housing projects, roads, hospitals, and so on, construction companies have an incentive to bribe those awarding these lucrative contracts or to pay off inspectors for accepting shoddy work.

This perspective on corruption has two implications. Some acts of corruption are good for economic efficiency because they undo the effects of bad laws—there may be, in some situations, an optimum level of bribery. Fees and permits to enter most businesses and occupations are simply barriers to entry that shield existing firms from competition. Bribes allow more firms or individuals to enter and are therefore good for competition and consumers.

Much corruption arises from government that intervenes more than necessary, taking as given the objectives of the intervention. Consider housing projects for the poor as an example. If government wants to help the poor afford housing, it can simply transfer income; this creates minimal scope for corruption. Alternatively, it could provide vouchers that constrain the income transfers to be spent on housing (see **vouchers versus**

redistribution in-cash or in-kind); this is also unlikely to generate corruption.

If government builds low-income housing projects, however, the scope for corruption is substantial. Unless government pays exactly the costs of construction, these projects are windfalls for the companies lucky enough to win the contracts, creating a motive for bribery. Thus a "smaller" government approach can minimize the chances of corruption.

The cure for corruption is therefore not stricter enforcement or more laws but less government. Creating new laws designed to prevent corruption just gives those affected even more incentive to pay bribes.

cost-benefit analysis

A standard cost-benefit analysis consists of a systematic accounting of the beneficial and deleterious impacts of a particular policy, including numerical estimates of the dollar value of each impact, added up to determine the overall difference between the value of the benefits and the value of the costs. In some contexts, it is possible to conduct exactly this kind of analysis. In certain business situations, for example, all the impacts of one decision versus another can be expressed in terms of revenues and costs.

When it comes to analyzing government policies, standard cost-benefit analysis is more difficult because the impacts of policies are difficult to quantify (e.g., how many lives might be saved by mandating baby car seats?) and hard to convert into dollar figures (e.g., what is the dollar value of saving the life of a two-year-old?). In some cases different people have opposite views about whether a particular impact is a cost or a benefit (e.g., increased drug use due to drug legalization), and intangible considerations (e.g., respect for the law) are virtually impossible to quantify.

The cost-benefit framework, broadly interpreted, is nevertheless the heart of the libertarian perspective on government policy. A good analysis should try to determine all the possible impacts of a given policy, think about which are beneficial versus harmful, and, to the extent possible, place some bounds on how large or small each cost or benefit might be. The libertarian claim is that this approach suggests much government does not pass a reasonable cost-benefit test.

The cost-benefit approach to analyzing policy does not always bring every reasonable person to the same conclusion. But it does force people on both sides of any issue to be explicit about their assumptions, providing a starting point for reasoned debate about policy.

criminal justice

Libertarians generally agree that government should ban actions like homicide, assault, robbery, and theft, plus expend resources for police, courts, and prisons that identify, prosecute, and incarcerate offenders.

That government should provide criminal justice services is not self-evident, however, at least from the viewpoint of this book. Private measures do and should play a role in reducing crime. Most people can limit their exposure to violence or theft through private mechanisms like locks, alarms, guard dogs, privately owned guns, and so on. Private provision of criminal justice might not be perfect, but as argued repeatedly here, that is not sufficient reason for government provision, since that provision comes with its own costs. Why is government provision of criminal justice different than the array of government interventions critiqued elsewhere?

Part of the answer is that government criminal justice attempts to prevent or punish actions, like violence and theft, that unequivocally harm someone. In contrast, many other government interventions seek to prevent voluntary interactions, where the presumption must be that a net benefit occurs from the private behavior.

A second part of the answer is that reducing the incidence of violence and theft is undeniably beneficial for society: Unless people feel secure in their person and property, the incentive to produce, invest, save, and innovate is too low, so productive activity grinds to a halt. This also contrasts with many government policies, where the goals of intervention, even if delivered, are debatable.

The final part of the answer is that provision of criminal justice is a classic public good: Everyone benefits if someone tracks down criminals and prevents them from committing further crime, yet no private party has a strong incentive to conduct such activities. Thus private provision of criminal justice might be less than is desirable over all.

Whether this underprovision is substantial enough to warrant government intervention is an empirical question, of course, but no society has survived without some government provision of criminal justice. Thus criminal justice is a case where the benefits from government provision seem likely to outweigh the negatives.

Yet the fact that provision of a criminal justice system is an appropriate activity for government in no way ensures that all actions of current criminal justice systems are beneficial—especially those that go beyond preventing and punishing violence or theft. Laws against vice, for example, prevent mutually beneficial exchange and generate their own negatives. Similarly, certain criminal justice procedures or policies, such as **capital punishment**, might be undesirable choices of how to punish criminals.

Note that the consequentialist libertarian defense of criminal justice is consistent with the rights-based libertarian defense of criminal justice. The latter view holds that the only appropriate role for government is defining and enforcing **property rights**. An individual's property includes his or her own person, along with any material goods, so laws against homicide, assault, or theft can be thought of as enforcing these property rights. The consequential and rights-based views are identical if defending these particular rights turns out to have good consequences, such as promoting a free and productive society.

democracy and capitalism

The United States expends considerable effort encouraging democracy around the world. While the United States also advocates capitalism, the tone of its policies is democracy first, capitalism second. The assumption is that democracy promotes beneficial outcomes such as freedom and economic growth, and that the most important freedoms are political ones—like the right to vote—rather than economic ones—like the right to property. This emphasis is backwards.

Democracies often adopt bad policies; everyone, regardless of political persuasion, can identify democratically adopted policies they abhor. In particular, fledgling democracies emphasize redistribution over efficiency. This is understandable, given that these economies do not have sizable middle classes, so redistribution looks, for most people, like a faster path to wealth than economic efficiency. Over a longer horizon, however, an overemphasis on redistribution shrinks the economic pie so much that almost everyone is worse off.

Attempts to install democracy distract attention from other issues that are crucial for a stable, growing economy—defining and enforcing property rights, establishing the rule of law, allowing foreign investment, maintaining free **trade**, privatizing government industries, limiting regulation, and avoiding **union** protections. All these policies are difficult to adopt or maintain under democracy, at least until a stable middle class exists.

The focus on democracy often addresses outward appearances of freedom such as holding elections or creating a constitution, rather than the fundamental components such as freedom of speech and religion, freedom to leave the country, and so on. Numerous totalitarian states have held elections without true freedom. At the same time, it is possible to have substantial freedom under a dictator.

More fundamentally, political freedom without economic freedom is impossible, and economic freedoms—to live where one wishes, to choose a school, language, or occupation, to merge with or buy other firms, to refuse to negotiate with unions, to hire replacement labor, and so on—matter greatly in their own right. All these freedoms promote the accumulation of private wealth and a strong middle class, and are thus key safeguards against oppressive government.

Whether or not emphasizing capitalism over democracy is advisable in principle, attempts to impose democracy rarely work. In places that do not have an appropriate level of income, a conducive historical tradition, or a stable middle class, or where religious and ethnic differences are deeply divisive, the temptation to undo democracy is huge. The more successful route to democracy appears to be to concentrate on economic development first and democracy itself second, once the necessary preconditions have gradually evolved.

disaster relief

In the aftermath of floods, hurricanes, earthquakes, and other natural disasters, governments often provide food, shelter, clothing, and medical care to the affected families. These transfers are compassionate, and it makes sense in principle for the members of a society to insure each other against these kinds of events.

Government provision of disaster relief can nevertheless be excessive and, in some cases, counterproductive. Certain natural disasters occur with a predictable frequency, and the prudent response is to avoid living or producing in the areas affected (e.g., beachfront property in hurricane zones). Government disaster relief can lower the costs sufficiently that populations locate in places where it does not make good economic sense. Indeed, in some instances government actively encourages this inappropriate risk taking by subsidizing hurricane insurance, or by building levees and dams to keep back the ocean, or by rerouting rivers that flood. If these efforts work imperfectly, as many do, government has then created a situation that is ripe for disaster.

A perfect illustration of these issues was the devastation of New Orleans by Hurricane Katrina in 2005. The areas that suffered the most extreme damage were portions of the city below sea level, an outcome made possible only because government had earlier built levees to keep back the sea from these areas. It is hard to imagine that any rational calculation could have suggested this as a good investment of the nation's resources. Land is not that scarce, so tempting Mother Nature—in an area with a high frequency of hurricanes—was insane. Worse, after Katrina decimated homes in low-income areas of the city, the government undertook to rebuild the levees and encourage resettlement. A more sensible and less expensive approach would have just given cash or vouchers to the displaced residents and allowed them to purchase houses elsewhere.

While government attempts to ameliorate natural disasters are liable to be excessive, private efforts are typically robust, especially in cases where truly unusual and horrific events have occurred. The right policy, therefore, is for governments to forgo disaster relief while not encouraging stupid risk taking in the first place.

discrimination

Discrimination on the basis of race, gender, religion, age, and so on has occurred throughout history and cultures. Modern societies condemn discrimination as morally abhorrent, and the most blatant forms of discrimination are less apparent now than in times past. Discriminatory attitudes and tendencies nevertheless persist, and many people assume discrimination would be rampant without government efforts to curtail it.

Consistent with this view, many governments seek to prevent discrimination and promote race and gender equality. The main policy is **bans on discrimination** in employment, lending, housing, college admissions, and other areas. In addition, **affirmative action** policies aim to encourage better treatment of protected groups. The main argument for these policies is that without government intervention, employers, lenders, academic institutions, and others would discriminate against minorities and women. An alternative argument for affirmative action is that anti-discrimination policies are necessary to remedy past discrimination, or to promote diversity in current organizations.

No reasonable person denies that discrimination occurs. Some people base this assessment on personal experience or casual observation. More generally, substantial race and gender differences persist in economic and social outcomes. These gaps seem to suggest that significant discrimination is still present in modern societies.

Differences across race or gender in education, wages, employment, and lending, however, can reflect factors other than discrimination. Because some minorities or women have fewer skills, creditworthiness, or other relevant characteristics, rational, non-discriminating employers or lenders might offer lower wages or loan rates based solely on these factors. Thus gaps in outcomes like wages or lending are not necessarily due to discrimination. If differences in underlying factors like skill or experience are substantial, and if policies that seek to reduce discrimination create their own negatives, then such policies may be inadvisable because they are pushing against economic decisions that are motivated by valid considerations, not discrimination.

In fact, discrimination is unlikely to be substantial in market economies because employers, lenders, universities, and others who discriminate put themselves at a competitive disadvantage. Employers who refuse to hire minorities or women face a smaller pool and must pay higher wages to attract a sufficient number of qualified employees. Banks that deny loans to creditworthy female borrowers lose business to other banks. Colleges that discriminate in admissions lose qualified students to non-discriminating schools. Even businesses that discriminate because they think their customers prefer it—such as restaurants that hire only white waiters—pay a price for this discrimination in higher wage costs and therefore resist such discrimination unless customers apply substantial pressure. Thus market forces help counter the discriminatory preferences of employers and others.

Existing evidence confirms that education, experience, creditworthiness, and, for women, withdrawals from the labor force for family reasons account for much of the observed differences in wage gaps or other differential outcomes between groups. Relatedly, increased education and experience for these groups have contributed substantially to the narrowing of these gaps over time. Thus, discrimination has played a significant role historically and continues to explain some of the differences across groups in economic and social outcomes, but this justification for anti-discrimination policies is easily overstated.

In fact, governments themselves have generated much discrimination. Slavery is the most extreme example. In the southern U.S. states, Jim Crow laws mandated segregation for decades. The Exclusion Act of 1882 barred Chinese immigration, and the federal government interned persons of Japanese descent during World War II. State universities historically excluded blacks and/or women. The U.S. military maintained separate units for blacks until 1948 and continues to exclude homosexuals via its "Don't Ask, Don't Tell" policy. Racial profiling has been used to enforce drug and immigration laws, and government-protected unions have excluded minorities and women. Apartheid in South Africa, a government system of discrimination against blacks and other non-white minorities, persisted for decades.

An alternate justification for anti-discrimination policies is that they can serve to correct past discrimination. Some minorities and women still suffer from historical discrimination, but this defense of intervention is problematic. Many women and minorities have succeeded despite past obstacles, long before the advent of government anti-discrimination policies. Some African-Americans are not descendants of slaves, so they did not experience the same magnitude of adverse treatment as African-Americans who are. Numerous ethnic, racial, and religious groups have been subject to discrimination (e.g., Asians, Irish, Jews, Eastern Europeans, Hispanics, Muslims, and so on), so deciding which groups to protect, or how much, is difficult. Every group, moreover, has had opportunities to remedy past discrimination, while many people in the "discriminating" groups did not themselves discriminate. Thus any attempt to compensate for past discrimination is hopelessly complicated. These efforts will over- or under-compensate and punish persons not guilty of discrimination.

The idea that anti-discrimination policies are necessary to promote diversity is also awkward because the appropriate definition of diversity is open to endless debate. Diversity might include all groups that have ever experienced significant discrimination, or only groups that experience substantial current discrimination. Diversity policies might promote only low-income or disadvantaged members of the targeted group, or everyone in that group. In practice diversity standards promote homogeneity of background, experience, or political views, since they tend to target successful members of minority groups, who typically resemble those defining and promoting diversity. Many minorities admitted to elite colleges for diversity reasons, for example, come from middle- or upper-class backgrounds.

Reasonable people can disagree over how much the differences across groups reflect discrimination, and over the importance of the arguments in favor of anti-discrimination policies. Whether or not these arguments are convincing, however, **bans on discrimination** and government-imposed **affirmative action** generate significant adverse consequences and may even increase discrimination.

disrespect for the law

Voluntary compliance with the law is a crucial condition for civil society because government cannot be everywhere without a ruinous commitment of resources. Thus government should not attempt to enforce laws that will experience wide-scale non-compliance, since that merely teaches everyone that laws are for suckers and that rules are made to be broken. Worse, enforcement of such laws is inevitably uneven, and thus people who obey the laws are hurt relative to those who do not; the honest suffer relative to the dishonest.

Prohibitions against vice are prime examples of policies that command only modest compliance and therefore reward the dishonest while generating disrespect for the law. Other such policies include speed limits, safety and health regulation, affirmative action, complicated tax codes, campaign finance regulation, environmental policies, and more.

This does not mean that all laws and regulations are bad. In some instances, government rules make sense even though violations will occur and some violators will avoid punishment. Laws against violence and theft are the best illustrations. These are the exceptions, however, and they differ from the cases discussed above. Laws against violence and theft do *not* forbid mutually beneficial exchange or interfere with purely voluntary actions, while vice prohibitions do. Similarly, laws against violence and theft do *not* mandate actions that affected individuals do not wish to undertake.

Instead, laws against violence and theft are meant to prevent harm to innocent third parties, so virtually everyone wants such laws to be obeyed. Thus, voluntary compliance with these laws, and with efforts to enforce them, is the norm.

drug prohibition

No one denies that drugs can harm users and society generally. Based on this fact, most societies have chosen to outlaw drugs like marijuana, cocaine, and heroin. The justification is that prohibition—a ban on production, distribution, and possession—reduces the harms from drug use. Prohibition may reduce drug use, but it is a terrible approach to reducing the associated harms.

Prohibition harms those who consume drugs despite prohibition. In addition to any negatives from drugs themselves, these individuals face the risk of arrest and imprisonment, along with the dangers of purchasing drugs in an underground market. Because prohibition raises drug prices, users have less income for food, shelter, clothing, and medicine. If drug prices were lower, as they would be in an open market, users could more productively spend their money on other services.

Prohibition also harms people who would be responsible users in a legal market but abstain due to prohibition. The benefit users obtain is a positive aspect of drug use, just as with other risky activities like downhill skiing, driving on the freeway, or betting on winners and losers in the stock market. The exact nature of this benefit varies across people; some use drugs for medicinal purposes, others to look cool, and still others because they enjoy being intoxicated. A free society takes as given that individuals are the best judges of what makes them better off, but prohibition impedes the ability to make these choices regarding drugs.

Because prohibition raises drug prices, users inject drugs to obtain the biggest bang-for-the-buck—thrift-minded users inject heroin, for example, rather than smoking opium, the less concentrated, precursor product from which heroin is made. Then, as a result of prohibition-induced restrictions on clean syringes, users share contaminated needles and spread blood-borne diseases such as hepatitis and HIV. This, in turn, puts a strain on public health facilities and charities that care for addicts, spreading costs to the rest of us. Thus, higher prices help spread disease and strain the health system.

Prohibition also reduces public health by encouraging medically unjustified limitations on therapeutic uses of marijuana, opiates, and other illegal drugs. The underground market also limits quality control, forcing users to face higher risks of overdoses or accidental poisonings; users in turn become a drain on the public health system. Legal products like alcohol are sold with labels that indicate purity, and cigarettes come with tar and nicotine ratings. Such products still carry health risks, but consumers have reasonable information about these risks and can therefore take steps to avoid or minimize them.

Prohibition erodes civil liberties. Crimes like robbery or assault generate a victim who complains to the police, but neither party to a drug transaction wants to alert authorities since both buyer and seller have broken the law. Thus police use intrusive tactics like warrantless searches or undercover buys—both of which infringe on civil liberties even as they fail to achieve their stated goal of reducing drug use. The victimless nature of drug crime gives police an excuse to engage in racial profiling since they can simply assert that minorities are more likely to use drugs.

Since it pushes drug markets underground, prohibition means participants cannot resolve disputes with lawyers or advertising, so they resort to violence instead. Violence was common in the alcohol industry during the years of alcohol Prohibition—but not before or after. Gambling markets were also marked by violence before state and federal governments legalized most forms. Likewise, violence occurs in prostitution markets mainly when prohibition forces these underground.

Prohibition enriches drug traffickers because the income earned in underground markets is not taxed (even as it produces the need for government expenditure). Prohibition corrupts politicians and law enforcement personnel because it threatens the livelihood of traffickers, who cannot lobby legislators or fund ballot initiatives to express their grievances.

Prohibition breeds **disrespect for the law** because no matter how draconian the penalties and how extensive the enforcement, many people still produce and use drugs. Everyone learns that laws are for suckers.

Prohibition harms the public purse because governments expend tens of billions of dollars on enforcement and forgo similar amounts in tax revenues not collected.

The right policy toward drugs is therefore legalization. In a legal regime, milder policies such as **sin taxes** or age restrictions might make sense, although these must be moderate to avoid the same negatives as prohibition.

Private mechanisms would also moderate the negatives of legalized drug use. Employee drug testing would discourage use both on and off the job, while competition and advertising would allow users to choose drugs with a high ratio of beneficial to adverse effects (e.g., coca tea rather than crack cocaine).

These conclusions about drug prohibition apply to alcohol, prostitution, gambling, consensual sexual activity, and pornography—any of the traditional vices. Prohibitions of consensual adult activity do little to reduce the negatives associated with these activities while creating black markets that have large, undesired side effects.

drunk driving laws

Driving under the influence of alcohol is illegal in most countries, and this policy plausibly reduces accidents. The policy therefore has a straightforward defense: reducing harm to innocent drivers, pedestrians, and property.

In contrast to policies like alcohol or **drug prohibition**, drunk driving laws target directly the behavior that negatively impacts third parties (i.e., **externalities**). This approach to addressing a social problem is therefore more likely to be beneficial than prohibition, which bans responsible use of drugs or alcohol and generates considerable unwanted side effects.

Thus drunk driving laws are acceptable to libertarians in principle. In some instances, however, drunk driving laws set the limit for intoxication so low that responsible, social drinkers get caught. In this case the policy consumes scarce police resources and does little to improve highway safety. This example thus illustrates how well-intentioned, sensible interventions can expand beyond the point at which they do more good than harm.

employee drug testing

One motivation offered for **drug prohibition** is that drug use allegedly lowers employee productivity. The evidence does not support this contention, but even if it did, this is not a convincing justification for prohibition. For employees, lower productivity results in lower wages, so individuals can decide for themselves whether to use drugs and earn less, or not. Furthermore, private remedies—namely, drug testing—could do a more effective job of figuring out which employees are using drugs, thereby giving employers the information they need to decide whom to hire and how much to pay. Thus drug testing of prospective or existing employees allows employers to avoid any negative productivity effects that might accompany drug use.

Policy should therefore not restrict private drug testing of employees. At the same time, neither should policy mandate testing, since that forces all businesses to incur these costs even if testing does not enhance productivity.

Policy toward employee drug testing provides a useful illustration of how the libertarian view differs from liberal and conservative perspectives.

Conservatives see drugs as undesirable and think government should reduce their use, so they think policy should mandate that employers subject their employees to drug testing. This approach stands in contrast to conservative rhetoric, which opposes regulation of business and holds that private decision makers do reasonable things when left alone.

Liberals see drug testing as an intrusion on privacy and want to restrict it in most private settings. Their view is that businesses will use testing to unfairly punish employees who use drugs, because liberals do not think competition in the labor market will set an appropriate wage differential for drug-using versus non-using employees. Liberals also do not see businesses as strictly private entities that deserve the freedom to run themselves as they see fit.

employer-provided health insurance

In the United States, much **health insurance** comes as an employer-provided fringe benefit. This occurs because, under the income tax code, employers can reduce their taxable profits by the premiums they pay on behalf of employees, but these employees do not have to treat the premiums as taxable income. Thus, employees end up with higher net-of-tax income if employers compensate them partially in the form of health insurance premiums.

This tax subsidy to health insurance means that most employed people buy more insurance than they would if faced with the full cost of the insurance. These people therefore demand more health care, which puts upward pressure on prices. Eliminating this distortion requires that the tax code treat employer payment of health premiums as taxable income to the employee. Then neither employees nor employers would have any reason for compensation to come in the form of health insurance, and the generosity of health insurance purchased would decrease. This reduction in health insurance would mean less **moral hazard** in the health care market and lower health care costs.

Elimination of the tax exemption for employer-paid health insurance premiums—which means higher tax collections if nothing else changes—allows for a decrease in some other tax that makes the overall change revenue-neutral. Assuming this decrease is for a tax that distorts economic incentives and reduces economic activity (e.g., the **personal** or **corporate income tax**), this change in the structure of taxation would therefore improve the efficiency of health care markets and make the tax code less distorting.

Elimination of the tax exemption without an accompanying reduction in some other tax is both a change in the structure of taxation and an increase in the amount, so whether it makes sense depends on the structure and level of other taxation and spending.

endangered species

Protecting endangered species is a popular environmental policy. The standard approach is to restrict the development of private property that is a habitat for the species in question. The U.S. Endangered Species Act, for example, has forbidden paper companies from cutting down forests that are home to particular owl species.

Preservation of endangered species may be a worthy goal, but restricting private development is a terrible way to accomplish it.

The first issue is that private markets provide adequate protection for endangered species that live in habitats where the **property rights** are well assigned. Individuals or businesses who value continued existence of such species can generate their preservation by purchasing the property and providing sanctuary for the relevant species. This applies whether the species has commercial value (e.g., bison) or emotional value (e.g., the bald eagle). If markets do not protect such species, it simply means that society does not place that much value on their continued existence. But that doesn't mean that individuals couldn't pay a premium for their preservation, if they really cared.

When a species lives in areas without well-defined property rights, markets do allow overly rapid depletion or even extinction. Those who suffer hard from extinction—future generations—cannot bribe the current generation into protecting the species. The ideal response in such situations, however, is to assign the relevant property rights. This gives the owners a long-run stake in the species and eliminates the need for transactions across generations. Selling off public lands, for example, gives private owners an incentive to protect species on these lands. Private game preserves in Africa are an example of this approach.

An alternative to the property rights approach is for society to compensate private property owners when development on their land is forbidden. This makes the costs of protecting species explicit and spreads the burden across all those who claim to value preservation. The number of species protected might be lower under this approach, since taxpayers would be faced with an explicit bill, but that is the right outcome. Restrictions on private development hide the costs of species preservation and thus lead to more protection than anyone is willing to pay for.

Even worse, attempting to protect species by forbidding development can be counterproductive. By preemptively converting a natural habitat to commercial use, owners can avoid losing the economic value of their property should authorities at some point decide it is home to an endangered species. Thus attempts to protect endangered species can in fact hasten their demise.

enforcing contracts

The ability to enter enforceable contracts is an essential ingredient of commercial and personal interactions. Private mechanisms generate some degree of contract compliance, since businesses and individuals who honor contracts develop reputations that are valued in the marketplace. Private mechanisms, though, may generate less compliance—and therefore fewer contracts—than is beneficial for society overall. Private mechanisms do not have the threat of force behind them, assuming the existence of standard laws that prohibit violence. Thus governments can plausibly enhance economic efficiency by providing courts that adjudicate contracts.

The view that government should help enforce *some* contracts does not imply government should enforce *all* contracts. The enforcement process utilizes resources (e.g., for judges and courtrooms), so government might want to refrain from enforcing contracts that are trivial (e.g., an agreement between two friends to wash each other's cars) or that involve minors (e.g., a deal between parent and child over doing the dishes) or that violate widely held notions of morality (e.g., a contract protecting slavery). The general rule, however, should be neutrality: governments should enforce all contracts that meet reasonable standards of clarity and enforceability, rather than choosing some kinds of contracts (e.g., mortgage debts) over others (e.g., gambling debts).

Contract enforcement can be viewed as one aspect of defining and enforcing property rights, since any agreement between two parties creates implicit claims on the current and future property of these parties. Thus a government role in contract enforcement is consistent with the libertarian view on **property rights**.

environmental policies

Protecting the environment is a critical issue in modern societies. Economic growth is essential to improved living standards, yet economic activity can generate air pollution, water pollution, and other damage. Economic development can also deplete nonrenewable resources such as oil and coal, endanger plant or animal species, or destroy green space and unique natural settings.

To address these adverse consequences of economic development, governments employ numerous policies that seek to protect the environment. Some mandate pollution-reducing equipment on industrial factories or emissions controls on automobiles. Others outlaw dumping of toxic wastes, require clean-up of lakes and rivers, protect the habitats of **endangered species**, or mandate **recycling** programs.

The standard argument for environmental policies relies on the concept of **externalities**. These occur when the actions of an individual or group impact third parties in ways *other* than market transactions. Pollution and other environmental impacts are classic examples of negative externalities. Driving a car generates emissions that affect everyone who breathes the air. Dumping toxic waste into a lake or river makes it less suitable for drinking or recreation, harming everyone who uses that body of water. Flying an airplane over a city creates noise that bothers residents.

When an activity generates an externality like pollution, society may view the activity as excessive because those engaging in the activity do not consider the costs they impose on others. Governments can potentially improve on market outcomes by discouraging activities that generate pollution or by regulating pollution itself. A tax on gasoline makes it more expensive to drive, which reduces driving and auto emissions. Requiring factories to treat their waste before dumping it in rivers limits the negative impact on water quality. Bans on late-night flights at airports can reduce the noise pollution imposed on nearby residents.

This argument for environmental policies is correct as far as it goes, but several caveats apply.

The externality argument suggests reducing activities that generate pollution—but not banning them entirely. Policy, for example, could eliminate auto emissions by banning cars, but that would impose far greater costs than any benefit from reduced air pollution. Thus moderate gasoline taxes or tolls on highways, which reduce driving and pollution without eliminating cars, are better approaches. The fact that some pollution exists or that some species become extinct does not mean environmental protection is insufficient.

Private contracting can sometimes reduce externalities without explicit environmental policies: Persons affected by externalities can pay the perpetrators to stop. A lakeside resort can pay an upstream factory to treat its waste, dump it elsewhere, or to move the factory. People who value the Northern

Spotted Owl can purchase the forest lands that harbor this species and maintain the forest in its native state.

Private resolutions to externalities do not always occur because of transaction costs (that is, any impediment to negotiation between the affected parties). A key cause of transaction costs is that the relevant **property rights** are not defined or enforced. A standard example is the air, which is why automobile emissions might easily be excessive unless government intervenes.

Thus assigning property rights is not always easy, but it can work. A classic example is the historical fencing-in of grazing areas, which allowed efficient use of these areas rather than the overuse that occurred without property rights. A more modern example is privatization of national parks in Africa, which has spurred protection of endangered wildlife because privatization has generated profits from eco-tourism. When government can assign property rights, this is the best approach to reducing externalities because it means all parties face appropriate incentives for efficient behavior.

A key factor in formulating good environmental policies is recognizing that tradeoffs exist between the environment and other resources. Preserving the environment has a benefit, but not an infinite one. This means that despite good intentions, environmental policies can do more harm than good (see **recycling** or **endangered species**). One mechanism for getting a reasonable balance is to leave environmental policies to the states rather than to the federal government (see **federalism**).

Much environmental degradation results from government policies. Some governments subsidize cutting down rain forests to encourage agriculture, ranching, or logging. Governments build dams, bridges, and roads that destroy natural habitats, including many instances where the benefits from these projects do not justify even their non-environmental costs. Governments own and lease huge tracts of land at below-market prices—for instance, for ranching in the western United States—which encourages excessive use. Thus one way to protect the environment is to avoid government policies that do not make sense in the first place.

estate tax

Most developed economies tax the wealth that is transferred at death from a deceased person to that person's heirs, a tax that stands in addition to the taxation that was applied to the income that produced this wealth. Estate taxation mainly targets large estates, but the rates imposed on such estates are often substantial (e.g., 40–50 percent or more). Some developed economies do not impose estate taxes (e.g., Australia, New Zealand, Sweden).

The usual justification for estate taxation is a desire to redistribute wealth. This seems punitive since the income that produced a given person's wealth has already been taxed, usually at progressive rates. Moreover, the estate tax has undesirable side effects.

The estate tax penalizes savings relative to spending. If a high-income individual saves most of the income earned over his lifetime, that savings and the accumulated interest get hit by the estate tax when passed on to an heir. If instead a high-income individual lives a lavish lifestyle and spends most of his income, his estate is smaller and incurs less tax. Taxation that punishes savings is exactly the opposite of what good economics suggests.

The estate tax generates compliance costs and wasteful avoidance behavior. High-income individuals hire lawyers to establish trusts that reduce estate taxes, for instance. The estate tax rewards dishonesty because it contains substantial scope for illegal but rarely detected evasion, such as overstating charitable donations or transferring income to heirs under the table.

The estate tax does not raise much revenue because those with large estates take appropriate avoidance steps, thereby reducing the amount of tax collected under the income tax. Many countries without an estate tax (e.g., Sweden) have more egalitarian income distributions than countries with an estate tax (e.g., the United States). Thus estate taxation accomplishes little from a distributional perspective yet generates substantial negatives.

externalities

Externalities occur when the actions of an individual or group impact third parties in ways *other* than market transactions, either positively or negatively. A standard example is pollution, as discussed under **environmental policies**, but externalities arise in a broad range of circumstances. Driving on the highway at rush hour imposes an externality because it slows the commute for everyone. Smoking or eating unhealthy foods imposes a "fiscal" externality by raising everyone's taxes in economies where government pays for health care. Externalities provide the grounds for a standard argument for government intervention.

When externalities exist, the allocation of resources is likely to be inefficient because those generating the externality (drivers during rush hour) do not account for the negative impacts their actions have on others (everyone else sits in traffic and breathes additional pollution). Government can improve the allocation of resources by reducing the activity that generates the externality. For example, highway tolls that are higher during rush hour cause some drivers to commute earlier or later, spreading the volume of traffic and reducing congestion.

The externality argument for government intervention is convincing in some instances, but a number of caveats apply.

To begin with, determining what constitutes an externality is difficult. Taking the next step and figuring out which ones society should reduce is doubly so. Washing one's laundry causes water pollution—a classic externality. Eating too much ice cream can cause heart disease, thereby increasing the costs of publicly funded health care. Watching late-night TV means less sleep and lower workplace productivity the next day, which can adversely affect one's co-workers. In other words, almost everything generates externalities. Since society does not have the resources to control them all, it must figure out which are most significant.

This complicated and subjective exercise often comes with problematic implications. Smoking, for example, causes elevated health costs, some of which are paid out of public funds. Thus, smoking causes a "fiscal" externality, and this might seem to justify policies to reduce smoking. At the same time, many smokers die younger than non-smokers, collecting less in Social Security and Medicare benefits—a positive fiscal externality because it reduces taxes on everyone else. The externality reasoning taken to its logical end thus implies that if smoking reduces Social Security and Medicare payments by more than it raises public health costs, governments should subsidize smoking.

Few people would endorse such a policy. Yet if society is unwilling to consistently apply the "spillover" logic of externalities, the concept becomes a tool of special interests who use it to promote their own goals. And rarely does the externality argument suggest banning the offending activity entirely. The fact that commuting to work imposes an externality does not mean policy should outlaw driving.

In some cases, private contracting can reduce externalities without government intervention. Persons affected by externalities can limit their exposure by paying those causing the externality to stop. Private contracting does not always occur due to impediments to negotiation between the affected parties: what economists call transactions costs. For example, owners of lakeside cottages who speak different languages might have difficulty reaching an agreement about the hours when power boats are allowed on the lake. A key cause of transaction costs is that **property rights** to the resource being affected are not defined or enforced. If no one has a clear title to the lake (or to "quiet on the lake"), then no one can easily write a contract that would implement the appropriate payments. The contracting approach is nevertheless successful in many instances.

See also **environmental policies.**

false or misleading advertising

Many societies ban false or misleading advertising as a way of protecting consumers. The usual assumptions behind this policy are that businesses use advertising to manipulate consumer preferences and that consumers are not sophisticated enough to see through excessive or false claims. It might seem obvious that policy should bar businesses from making false or misleading claims, but in practice this policy is deleterious.

Little evidence supports the assumption that advertising gets consumers to buy things they do not want. Throughout history, highly advertised products have flopped in the marketplace.

Even if advertising were persuasive, private mechanisms can provide independent information about product quality. Businesses advertise the ratings they receive from independent rating agencies. Consumers who value quality ensure that good products survive, and naïve consumers just follow along. Competitors cry foul or run counter-advertising when another firm makes exaggerated claims for its products. In this kind of war of words, consumers benefit from additional information and can vote for a product with their wallets, providing a signal to other consumers. More such information would arise if firms were not concerned that aggressive claims invite punishment from regulators. In effect, government regulation reduces information for consumers.

Even if advertising does persuade some consumers to buy products they do not want, and even if some advertising relies on false or misleading claims, policies that restrict advertising have their own negatives.

Much advertising provides useful information about new products and their features. This information is valuable to consumers, and no plausible regulation can limit persuasive advertising without also limiting informative advertising. Firms with new or improved products use advertising to compete, but this mechanism is less effective if firms worry about misstatements. Thus advertising restrictions are bad for competition.

Restrictions on advertising are infringements of free speech. Existing jurisprudence in the United States holds that commercial speech does not deserve the same legal protection as political speech, but this distinction is meaningless. Earning a living is a crucial freedom, and advertising helps many people earn a living. Indeed, technologies like the Internet make it difficult for governments to restrict freedom, and advertising is one mechanism that supports the Internet. Commercial speech is therefore an important protector of the freedoms safeguarded by political speech.

Regulating advertising also encourages people to be careless in making their purchases. If policy asserts it has banished false and misleading advertising, naïve consumers accept advertising claims at face value. In truth, government cannot monitor more than a tiny fraction of advertising, nor would it be easy to decide which ads are good or bad, even if the resources were available (think about phrases like "promotes healthy living," "makes skin act younger," or "may decrease cholesterol"). Thus policy cannot immunize consumers against unscrupulous firms. Consumers must use common sense, which is more likely in a world where policy does not give false assurances.

Market forces, moreover, can and do punish businesses that make unwarranted claims. Companies whose products are harmful earn bad reputations and lose business. For example, lack of consumer demand, not government regulation, drove the Edsel and New Coke out of the marketplace.

A different mechanism that disciplines firms is the **product liability** system, which allows consumers to sue for damages from defective products. This system has its own problems, but it makes sense in moderation and provides a check on business behavior. Under product liability, businesses recognize that excessive or false claims expose them to punishment that might offset any benefit from misleading consumers.

Thus, even in the case of extreme behavior—explicitly false claims made by firms to promote their products—policies that attempt to protect consumers are worse than the disease.

federalism

Provision of national defense and laws against treason are inherently national policies and thus should be conducted by a federal government. But for most policies, societies have a choice: They can conduct policy at the federal level or leave policy to state and local governments. For much of U.S. history, for example, education policy was the province of state and local governments; only in the 1960s did the federal government adopt policies that modify state education policies or provide additional funding, with the 2002 adoption of No Child Left Behind making this shift in power virtually complete. **Abortion** policy was a state matter until *Roe v. Wade*, and most **criminal justice** is still state rather than federal.

The trend in the United States over the past century has been for increasing federal involvement in matters previously left to states. The standard argument for federal control assumes that the appropriate interventions are similar across states and that, left to their own devices, states will not intervene enough. The specific fear is that states will engage in a "race to the bottom" in which each state chooses the least possible intervention to keep taxes low and avoid scaring away businesses.

In fact, state-level intervention makes more sense than federal intervention in all but a few cases, if intervention is necessary at all. Having states set policy allows for variety and innovation. In education, for example, some states might employ public schools while others experiment with vouchers or charters. This experimentation provides useful information for all states.

A different benefit of federalism is reduced **polarization**. If each state sets its own policy toward gay marriage, for example, states with strong support will be more likely to legalize while those opposed will be less likely. This outcome is unsatisfactory to those who support gay marriage, but it means legalization can proceed at a pace that is consistent with local norms. Forcing gay marriage on states that do not yet support it risks a backlash.

Federal control makes sense only if the appropriate intervention is similar across states or if the federal government can easily adjust its rules for different states. Neither condition is more than rarely met; another reason state control makes sense. Even in cases where the policy of one state affects the residents of another state (e.g., pollution that crosses state lines, such as acid rain), states can negotiate with each other to mitigate these effects.

In addition, many interventions expand past the point where the costs exceed the benefits (see **slippery slopes**). When a federal or national government conducts policy, nothing counters the tendency toward overexpansion. When a state sets policy, however, it must worry that excessive regulation could drive consumers or businesses into other states. Thus, leaving policy to the states provides a counterbalance to the tendency toward excess, while allowing individual states, if they wish, to impose policies that are more restrictive than federal mandates.

Beyond these considerations, the U.S. historical experience does not indicate that a race to the bottom usually occurs. The United States transferred control of welfare to the states in 1996, and the outcome was a moderation but hardly a gutting of welfare. During the 1920s and early 1930s, and before the federal government created Social Security, many states adopted their own old-age assistance programs despite the risk of becoming welfare magnets. States, moreover, routinely adopt policies more generous than any federal mandate, such as minimum wages above the federal level, higher levels of unemployment insurance, broader coverage under Medicaid, funding of stem cell research, and more restrictive environmental policies, to name a few. Thus states exhibit altruism, which counters the race to the bottom.

fiscal stimulus

One way that governments attempt to avoid or reduce recessions is by increasing the level of government spending, or decreasing the level of taxes, when a recession is imminent or underway. The additional spending includes infrastructure, education, energy, research and development, and in some cases, the military. The tax cuts include reductions in employment taxes, personal income taxes, and corporate income taxes.

The case for a spending stimulus relies on two separate lines of argument. One holds that government spending should be higher based on standard cost-benefit considerations. Private businesses, for example, might not build all the roads that would be efficient because acquiring the property rights is complicated. Thus, independent of the need to simulate the economy, governments should build more roads. A recession is merely what generates the political will to commit the tax revenues.

The cost-benefit argument for fiscal stimulus is reasonable in some instances; when the government has projects that correct market failures, and can implement them without generating excessive side effects, it should do them. If this happens to coincide with a recession, that is fine. Further, the costs of resources like labor are low during recessions because of high unemployment, so the optimal timing of government projects might be counter-cyclical—that is, government gets the most bang for its buck in bad times.

The cost-benefit argument for fiscal stimulus is nevertheless wildly overstated in most circumstances because virtually all kinds of government expenditure are too high, not too low, on cost-benefit grounds. A few exceptions to this rule of thumb exist, and a century ago the set of beneficial projects was plausibly higher than now (e.g., some highways). In modern economies, however, the examples of excess spending vastly outnumber the examples of insufficient spending, so it is hard to make the case for fiscal stimulus on these grounds.

The alternative argument for fiscal stimulus is the traditional Keynesian analysis in which government spending causes increased private spending, which then multiplies through the economy. This view is plausible under certain assumptions, but it faces two obstacles. First, existing evidence has not made a good case for the prediction that an extra dollar of government spending generates more than a dollar of overall income. Second, the analysis explicitly ignores any cost-benefit criterion for the spending, so it implies that paying people to dig ditches and fill them up is good for the economy.

This makes no sense in the long run, since at that point increased government spending crowds out private economic activity. Yet many government projects last for decades after recessions have ended, so, unless these projects make sense in cost-benefit terms, any additional spending is harmful over the long haul.

Tax cuts are a much better form of stimulus because they transfer purchasing power from government to taxpayers, so choices about spending devolve to individuals rather than bureaucrats. Even better, reductions in tax rates—as opposed to just fixed tax credits—increase economic efficiency by reducing the distortions caused by high rates. An ideal method of stimulus would be repeal of the **corporate income tax**, since this makes sense independent of the state of the economy.

See also **central banks and monetary policy, Great Depression, stabilization policies, taxes.**

fixed versus flexible exchange rates

The value of a given currency in world markets is known as the exchange rate, the price of foreign currency measured in units of the domestic currency. For example, the dollar/euro exchange rate is the dollar price of a euro.

Every country must decide between two exchange rate regimes. One system a country can adopt, known as flexible (or floating) exchange rates, is to let the market determine the value of its currency. Thus, when the demand for dollars changes relative to the demand for euros, the dollar price of euros changes. Under a strict floating regime, government agencies like the central bank or Department of the Treasury never buy or sell the domestic currency in foreign exchange markets.

A different approach, known as fixed exchange rates, requires a government agency like the central bank or Treasury to choose a particular value for the currency in terms of other currencies. To maintain this price, the agency must maintain stocks of foreign currency and stand ready to buy and sell at the official price. Since this agency is always willing to buy or sell unlimited amounts at this price, no transactions ever occur at a different price.

Flexible exchange rates make more sense than fixed exchange rates because they allow the market to determine the exchange value of the currency. The negatives associated with exchange rates, such as currency and balance-of-payments crises, occur when a country is about to run out of foreign currency reserves, implying it can no longer maintain a fixed exchange rate. This can only happen under fixed rates. Under flexible rates, the exchange value of the currency simply adjusts to changes in demand and supply.

flat tax

Most economies that utilize a personal income tax system adopt a progressive structure, which means the tax rate increases as the amount of income a taxpayer earns increases. For example, a person earning $50,000 per year might pay $10,000 in taxes while a person earning $100,000 per year might pay $30,000. The higher-income person not only pays more ($30,000 versus $10,000) but also a higher percentage (30 percent versus 20 percent). Progressive taxation thus redistributes from higher to lower income taxpayers.

An alternative to a progressive income tax is a flat tax, a system that applies the same tax rate to every dollar of income, regardless of the overall amount of income earned. Under a flat tax of, say, 10 percent, a taxpayer with $100 in income would pay $10 in taxes; a taxpayer with $100,000 in income would pay $10,000; and a taxpayer with $1 million in income would pay $100,000.

The flat tax approach has three virtues. The first is simplicity. Because every dollar earned pays the same rate, taxpayers have an easy time knowing how much extra tax they owe from expending different amounts of effort to earn income. A flat tax also avoids distortions that arise in real-world tax systems, such as the marriage penalty (the extra tax two people with significantly different incomes pay if married compared to what they would pay, combined, if single).

The second advantage of a flat tax is that since all income is taxed, the rate can be lower for any given amount of revenue collected. This means that high-income taxpayers do not face extreme tax rates, and this improves the incentive to work and save.

The third benefit of a flat tax is that it requires all taxpayers to "have some skin in the game," that is, to realize that an increase in government expenditure will affect their tax liability. Because progressive tax systems can exempt people who make less than a given amount from all tax, taxpayers below this cutoff view increased government expenditure as free because they will not personally bear any additional taxation to pay for it.

The main criticism levied at a flat tax is that it requires people with low incomes to pay positive amounts in taxes. A natural way to address this is by incorporating a **negative income tax**, which would guarantee a minimum income while taxing earned income at the flat rate. This would make the tax system progressive: Taxpayers with higher incomes would pay a higher fraction of their income in taxes, but everyone would still have to face a positive tax rate. The degree of progressivity would depend on the guaranteed level of income in the negative income tax. Thus, a system with this structure can accomplish reasonable distributional goals without great cost, assuming the guaranteed level of income is not too high.

foreign aid

Developed countries often provide economic and humanitarian aid to developing countries. Sometimes this aid comes with the requirement that the receiving country follow suggested economic policies, but sometimes it has no explicit strings attached.

The track record of aid coupled with policy prescriptions is poor, although this is less puzzling than some make it out to be.

Developed countries have difficulty running their own econo-mies, so it is not shocking their advice to developing countries is frequently off the mark. Even when the advice makes sense, developing countries do not necessarily follow it.

Foreign aid that is not conditioned on specific policies might seem to be unambiguously beneficial for the receiving country, but unrestricted aid distracts attention from desirable policy changes that countries could adopt on their own. In fact, past experience indicates that foreign aid does little to help devel-oping countries and might even contribute to worse outcomes. Many African and Latin American countries have been major recipients of aid for decades, yet most of these economies con-tinue to stagnate.

funding scientific research

Most developed economies subsidize scientific research through grants to individuals and universities and by operating systems of higher education.

The standard justification for this funding rests on three claims. The first is that basic science is not a marketable prod-uct because it is too fundamental or abstract. The second is that once basic research exists, everyone can readily copy it, so basic science cannot earn a financial return even when the ideas eventually lead to profitable products; if this is so, no market mechanism will produce basic science. The third claim is that applied science—the kind that generates marketable products and therefore profits—flows from basic science. Thus, if markets fail to produce basic science, applied science and technological innovation suffer.

These claims are plausible in many instances, but government funding of science is problematic.

Many scientists have in fact produced basic research despite the difficulty of capturing a financial gain (Galileo, Newton, Descartes, Darwin, Pasteur, Adam Smith, Milton Friedman). Private universities support basic research, in part because they believe it is good for society, in part because it is synergistic with educating their students. Philanthropists also fund basic science.

Private businesses produce basic research, despite what might seem to be insufficient financial incentives. Funding basic research is one way to compensate top scientists whose main interest is basic rather than applied science. By allowing cutting-edge scientists to pursue basic as well as applied topics, businesses get them out of academia and involved with applied topics. This benefits the company by putting great minds to work on issues that may generate profitable innovations. The company can also gain a competitive advantage by being the first to utilize a new idea, even when pure science becomes common knowledge once incorporated into marketable products.

The case for government funding is also not compelling because much applied research stems from existing applied research, not from basic research. In fact, applied research often inspires pure research by producing empirical regularities that pure science then explains.

These theoretical issues aside, the evidence suggests government funding has minimal impact on technological progress. U.S. productivity has proceeded at a steady pace for two centuries, yet significant government funding for science occurred only during the last 60 years. Thus, whatever the merits of the arguments about how scientific progress ought to work, the degree to which private forces underfund science does not appear to be large. In addition, government funding has harmful side effects.

The fundamental problem is that if government funds science, it must choose which science to fund. This means politics, rather than science, can determine the choices: Right-to-life supporters oppose government funding of stem cell research, lobbyists for specific diseases promote spending that is disproportionate to the incidence of the disease, all manner of research masquerades as being about the environment, and any research that appears to support drug prohibition—or the war on terror—gets funded.

Government funding centralizes decisions about which science to fund, yet government research panels make mistakes that have a major influence because of government's dominant role. Government funding can thus perpetuate a bias toward big science, because the projects chosen generate pork that politicians can dole out, or toward the status quo, because government funding faces little competition. Much of what government funds, including economics research, is interesting but irrelevant. Government often funds applied science, such as biotechnology, even though industry has ample incentive to undertake such research without subsidy.

Beyond these effects, government funding of science legitimizes an argument that is easily abused, namely, that because a particular activity generates a benefit that private parties cannot capture, society should fund this activity to get the socially optimal amount. The argument sounds reasonable, but advocates of subsidy can apply it to almost anything, from baseball stadiums to golf courses to symphony orchestras.

So while the social spillover argument is logical and sometimes correct, society should be wary because it is easily overextended. If a benevolent and thoughtful dictator were choosing what science to fund, the beneficial effects might outweigh the deleterious ones. This, however, is not the way things work.

gambling

During much of U.S. history, state governments typically barred most or all forms of gambling. These legal restrictions have weakened enormously over the past several decades, and most state governments now actively promote gambling via their state lotteries.

The arguments against gambling bans are similar to those against **drug prohibition**. These bans do little to reduce gambling, and they generate underground markets that are corrupt and violent.

Rather than operating lotteries, state governments could legalize all gambling and then impose a **sin tax,** that is, a tax on gambling services that is higher than other tax rates. It is not obvious that gambling generates adverse effects that might justify a sin tax; most of the negatives associated with gambling—crime, corruption—result from gambling prohibitions, not gambling per se. The sin tax approach, however, at least raises this debate explicitly instead of sweeping it under the rug through government's monopoly pricing of state lotteries. The lottery approach is also awkward because it puts government in the position of appearing to support an activity that some people regard as vice.

gays in the military

The United States and other countries have historically banned gay men and women from serving in their armed forces. Some countries continue this practice (e.g., Brazil, Cuba, China, Iran, Saudi Arabia, Turkey), but over the past several decades many have changed their policies to allow gay men and women to serve openly and without harassment (e.g., Australia, Canada, Germany, Israel, Italy, the United Kingdom, Switzerland). The United States still bans openly gay men and women but in principle allows gays to serve secretly under its "don't ask, don't tell" policy.

The usual argument made for excluding gays from the military is that, because of anti-gay sentiment among some non-gay soldiers, the presence of gays might undermine cohesion and discipline. No evidence, however, supports this view; gays have served with minimal problems in numerous countries. The same arguments made against gays in the military were offered decades ago in the United States to oppose racial integration of the armed forces, yet these forces are now entirely integrated with minorities disproportionately represented.

The correct policy, therefore, is for the United States to repeal its "don't ask, don't tell" stance, as well as to eliminate any federal prohibition on gay service. Whether a U.S. policy should compel the armed forces to allow gays to serve openly—or just leave the issue to the individual armed forces—is a more subtle question. A decentralized approach might lead to slower change, but it might also produce a less **polarizing** transition.

global warming

Debate will likely continue on the underlying science of global warming, including the question of how much warming is occurring and to what extent it is human-made. Even if those questions become fully resolved, however, most policies that aim to address warming are hard to justify.

The first reason for caution is that warming is not necessarily harmful, or at least is substantially less harmful than portrayed by advocates of new policies. Some parts of the planet are currently colder than is desirable, even while other parts might become too warm due to higher temperatures. Some ports will diminish in quality as sea levels rise, but others will become more suitable. Some land that is currently fertile for agriculture might become less productive, but other land that is currently too cool might become more hospitable. Thus, because of these trade-offs, the net effect of warming may be small. Assuming this warming occurs over the time horizon predicted by existing climate models, moreover, societies have ample time to adjust gradually rather than being forced to accommodate higher temperature quickly.

The second reason to go slowly on new policies is that many existing policies, already undesirable in their own right, encourage the use of fossil fuel and thereby contribute to greenhouse gas emissions. Before enacting costly new policies, it makes sense to eliminate existing bad policies that are contributing to the problem.

The set of such policies is large. In many countries government keeps the price of gasoline or heating oil well below its market price, which is the opposite policy of what global warming concerns suggest. Governments prevent public and private utilities from using peak-load pricing—prices that are higher at times of the day or week when demand is highest—which reduces the efficiency of energy or electricity generation and requires more pollution and burning of fossil fuel. Similar considerations apply to toll roads, where the absence of peak-load pricing means excessive congestion and wasted energy as commuters sit in traffic jams. Ethanol subsidies, designed to reduce the burning of fossil fuel, are enormously expensive and appear to increase greenhouse gas emissions when farmers convert ecosystems to production of biofuels such as corn.

The final reason to question global warming policies is that these policies will do little to reduce warming and yet impose enormous costs. Existing analyses suggest that virtually every policy so far advocated—Kyoto, cap and trade, carbon taxes—either has minimal impact or creates large distortions, or both. It makes more sense to spend the same money in other ways, such as slowing the spread of malaria or improving the education systems in developing countries.

gold standard versus fiat money

Every economy chooses a kind of money. Historically, many used a commodity money, such as coins made from gold or silver, but in modern times most utilize fiat money, which means pieces of paper that are intrinsically worthless but that trade in commerce because everyone believes they have value.

Many libertarians believe that a commodity money, such as gold, is superior to fiat money. Their principal argument is that governments can expand the stock of fiat money at virtually no cost, which then leads to periods of high and volatile inflation. Under a commodity standard, the government's ability to expand is limited by the existing supplies of the commodity, so government cannot expand freely and inflation stays in check.

This argument for a gold standard is defensible in principle, but the reality is less reassuring. Governments can expand the money stock under a gold standard by debasing the currency (changing the ratio of base metal to gold in its coins) or by devaluing gold (changing the ratio of gold coins to paper money). Governments can decree that additional metals constitute part of the currency. Governments can abandon a gold standard entirely. Thus, nothing guarantees that a government operating under a gold standard cannot generate major fluctuations in the money supply.

A different negative of a gold standard is the opportunity cost of the gold used as money. Precious metals used as money are not available for jewelry, statues, and so on. This is perhaps a minor issue if a gold standard in fact improves the conduct of monetary policy, but it is a cost nevertheless.

In practice, gold standards have often worked badly. The reluctance of many economies to abandon gold is widely considered a key reason for the depth of the Great Depression. The U.S. inflation rate varied considerably in the 19th century under a gold standard, in part because random discoveries of gold changed the quantity available. Political demands for inflation that would relieve debt burdens on farmers were a major source of uncertainty about the path of money.

More broadly, a gold standard is an attempt by government to tie its own hands and thereby avoid discretionary changes in the money supply that might cause inflation or otherwise perturb the economy. As with other attempts to limit policy discretion with an institutional arrangement (e.g., independent central banks, balanced budget amendments, trust funds, and lock boxes), this attempt is likely to fail. So long as political pressures exist for bad behavior, government typically finds a way to respond, regardless of the institutional constraints. Worse, pretending that one has solved a problem with an institutional fix can generate a false sense of security and distract from addressing fundamentals.

In the case of the money supply, the key problem is that government has control of the money supply, not the fact that this supply is gold versus fiat money.

See also **central banks and monetary policy**.

Great Depression

Between 1929 and 1933, the U.S. economy contracted by almost one-third. The depressed state of economic activity persisted for over a decade: unemployment exceeded 10 percent, and frequently 20 percent, and the level of output did not regain its 1929 level until 1939.

Much criticism of free markets points to the Great Depression as evidence that capitalist economies are excessively volatile and prone to severe contractions unless monetary and fiscal policies are used to dampen fluctuations.

In fact, much of the huge decline in output, as well as the length of the downturn, reflected policy mistakes rather than failures of private markets. Congress enacted large tariff increases in 1930, which generated retaliatory tariffs that shrank world trade. Congress adopted major tax increases, the opposite of what counter-cyclical fiscal policy should have done. The Federal Reserve allowed the money stock to fall dramatically, again the opposite of sensible policy. Both the Hoover and Roosevelt administrations proposed or implemented policies designed to protect unions, raise real wages, and reduce competition in industry, a recipe for economic disaster. More broadly, both administrations proposed so many new policies that the private sector faced great uncertainty just due to government's reaction to the economy; this uncertainty almost certainly contributed to the slowdown.

Rather than demonstrating that active policy is beneficial, therefore, the Great Depression is a textbook case showing that intervention can make things worse.

gun control

Policies that restrict or outlaw guns include waiting periods to buy a gun, mandatory background checks on those who purchase a gun, registration systems, age limits, concealed carry laws, and limits on the kinds of guns that can be legally sold. The usual argument asserts that guns cause crime and that controls, by reducing availability, reduce crime. Both pieces in the argument are flawed.

Many crimes do not require an armed perpetrator, and numerous weapons can substitute for guns (knives, baseball bats, fists, bombs, chains, shivs—the list is endless). Even if guns encourage or facilitate crime, guns potentially prevent crime by giving criminals reason to worry that victims might shoot back. In addition, policy cannot make guns disappear; it can only attempt to reduce availability via regulation, taxation, or prohibition. Those with illegitimate purposes, however, can circumvent such policies by borrowing or stealing a gun, or purchasing one on the black market.

Existing evidence confirms that the availability of guns plays a small role in causing crime and that gun control does little to reduce crime. Numerous countries have widespread gun ownership but low crime or violence rates; other countries have strict gun control laws but abundant guns and substantial violence. Police stations, army barracks, and rural households have high gun prevalence but little crime. Simply stating that guns automatically lead to high levels of crime is facile.

In addition, gun controls have costs, both for individuals and for society. Many people derive a benefit from owning guns. Some enjoy collecting, others like hunting or target-shooting, and others want guns for self-defense. Controls raise the costs of gun ownership, thereby harming legitimate users. The costs of many of these controls are mild—a three-day waiting-period to buy a gun, for example, imposes small costs on those with legitimate reasons to own a gun. Yet such controls do little to deter illegitimate uses, so they also have minimal benefits.

The potentially significant cost of mild controls is that they evolve into strict controls. A century ago no country had substantial controls on gun ownership, yet most now have strict controls or virtual prohibition. If gun control becomes prohibition, the potential for adverse effects is large. Prohibition creates black markets, which means violent dispute resolution, corruption of judges and police, and disrespect for the law.

Such outcomes are easily worse than any negatives of guns themselves.

The most significant negative of gun control is distracting attention from policies like **drug prohibition** that play a far larger role in generating crime. So long as policy generates a demand for crime, policy can do little to reduce crime.

health care costs

Some argue that the government should intervene in health care because of rising costs. Increasing expenditure on health care, however, is not necessarily a problem. As societies get richer, the desired composition of consumption spending changes. For items like food, clothing, and shelter, increased expenditure beyond a certain level is likely to produce relatively small gains in happiness. Many persons, however, want to spend a higher fraction of their rising income on health, since better health enhances enjoyment of everything else. Thus increasing health care expenditure is a problem only if it results from incentives for excessive purchases of health care. The most likely source of perverse incentives is government subsidies for health insurance.

In fact, health care is not necessarily getting more expensive. Rather, medical technology is constantly progressing, so health care is improving in quality. This often means higher prices, at least in the short run, but the cost of any given drug, treatment, or procedure is constant or falling. Indeed, in many cases quality has risen dramatically. Cataract surgery is a good example. Decades ago this surgery required a significant stay in the hospital and was only moderately effective. It is now done on an outpatient basis, and the success rate is extremely high. The price has risen, but by far less when weighted against the improvements in quality.

Thus much of the concern about rising health care costs is based on an erroneous assumption. Increasing health care costs are a problem for government budgets, of course, whether or not they reflect improved quality, because the higher expenditure requires higher taxes. The obvious way to address this issue is for governments to subsidize **health insurance** to a lesser degree (e.g., by phasing in a higher age of eligibility for old-age health insurance programs like Medicare).

One specific area in which claims about increasing costs have been particularly common is prescription drugs. As with medical care generally, this concern is misplaced. Costs are stable or declining for existing drugs; the high prices for new drugs represent improvements in quality. The unfortunate consequence of government prescription drug coverage is that, due to technological progress, it is inevitable that expenditure under such a program will rise. This creates pressure for price controls, which then depress the incentive for development of new drugs.

health insurance

Everyone cares about health and longevity, and modern societies expend enormous resources on health care. Conventional wisdom holds, however, that health care is different from other goods and cannot, or should not, be provided solely by private markets: It is too important for the government not to get involved. According to this view, health expenditures are large and unpredictable, and markets do not provide affordable health insurance. Unsurprisingly, given these views, most countries provide below-cost health insurance or subsidize the purchase of private insurance.

The arguments for subsidizing health insurance boil down to one of two claims. The first is that private markets do not supply health insurance efficiently due to a phenomenon called adverse selection (see **asymmetric information and adverse selection**). The second is that even if health insurance markets work well, health insurance will be prohibitively expensive for many people. Thus, governments should subsidize as a way to help the poor. Doing so will improve the overall health of the society.

The claim that private markets do not provide fairly priced insurance rests on the assumption that insurers cannot tell who is a good or bad risk (this is the problem of asymmetric information). Insurers must therefore charge everyone the same premium. In this case only the unhealthy find insurance worth purchasing, so insurers whose premiums reflect the average risk-level go broke (they get an adverse selection of customers). Recognizing this problem, insurers exit the market or charge a premium consistent with the high risk group. Low-risk consumers purchase either no health insurance or too little and must purchase health care on a fee-for-service basis. These consumers suffer a loss because the risks associated with health expenditures are not diversified away by being pooled with those of other people.

A potential response to the adverse selection problem is for government to force everyone to purchase insurance at a price that just allows insurance companies to make a fair return on average. Under this condition, the insurance programs balance financially (the premiums received by companies exactly equal the expenditure paid out, plus a fair return), and everyone gets insurance.

The adverse selection argument is not convincing. The key assumption is that consumers know their own health better than insurance companies. For example, consumers allegedly have private information about pre-existing medical conditions or behaviors that affect health such as exercise, sleep, or smoking. In fact, insurance companies can learn anything they want to know about insurance applicants by requiring stress tests, EKGs, blood tests, and other diagnostic procedures that predict future health. Insurers, moreover, have more experience evaluating health records than a typical individual and a strong incentive to be accurate in their assessments. Additionally, insurers can condition coverage on refraining from smoking, or getting regular exercise and checkups, or taking appropriate medications (assuming no legal limitations on these kinds of contracts).

Thus, the real issue for health insurance is that people with poor health might face high prices for insurance. This then raises the concern that government should subsidize insurance as a way to help the poor. The fact that some people cannot afford health insurance does not, however, mean government should provide it. If society wishes to help the poor, government can simply transfer income and let the recipients use this income to purchase health insurance. Transferring income in the form of health insurance might make sense for paternalistic reasons in the case of children in poor families, or perhaps for the poor more generally, but that is a separate issue.

Subsidizing health insurance does not therefore have a convincing justification. In addition, it generates its own negatives.

The first problem with subsidizing insurance is that, once insured, people adjust their behavior because they face a small or zero cost of health care. This **moral hazard** means that some people demand more care or even engage in less healthy behavior than they would if they paid the full price. Likewise, doctors recommend extra procedures and diagnostic tests, partially to avoid liability but also because patients who do not pay the full cost are insensitive to price. Thus insurance means that the prices decision-makers face in health care markets do not reflect the full costs of their decisions, so they demand more than is socially desirable.

The fact that insurance generates moral hazard is inescapable; it occurs under any private or public system. Private insurance policies, however, attempt to moderate moral hazard via co-payments, deductibles, and coverage limitations. Many government programs exclude these, which makes the moral hazard problem worse.

A second issue is that subsiding or mandating insurance requires government to choose a specific insurance policy, but this is messy. Ideal insurance covers large, unexpected expenses related to conditions over which those insured have no control, such as a pre-existing condition like Huntington's disease; ideal insurance does not cover conditions that people can avoid, such as lung cancer caused by smoking, or that are not crucial determinants of health, such as fertility treatments or some kinds of cosmetic surgery. A well-designed system would also limit coverage for treatments with indifferent success, such as some medications for mental illness. In short, ideal insurance is complicated.

Governments are not typically adept at handling messy, complicated issues; they do not make careful tradeoffs but instead provide insurance plans that are broad. This alleviates the need to make the hard decisions about what to cover, and it responds to political pressure for more rather than less coverage. But the result is excessive use of health care resources and extreme exacerbation of moral hazard.

A different problem is that mandating or subsidizing health insurance generates nonproductive behavior in health care markets as people respond to the incentives created by the policy. Under such programs, the government must set prices at which it reimburses health care expenses. Otherwise, providers will set arbitrarily high prices, knowing they get reimbursed by government.

Setting the right prices is difficult. If the government sets prices below market levels, doctors and hospitals will not supply medical services or will engage in rationing, fraud, creative accounting, and other non-productive behavior to recover their costs. Likewise, squeezing reimbursements for doctors and hospitals reduces the incentive for innovation. Further, if governments set prices that are not equivalent for alternative kinds of medical care (e.g., surgery versus medication to treat a particular condition), this creates incentives for treating conditions in ways that are not medically ideal and for billing practices that attempt to maximize reimbursements. If the government sets market prices, it faces ever-increasing expenditure as technology improves and more expensive medical care becomes available. This conflict between expensive medical care and the political desire to limit expenditure becomes worse over time.

The bottom line is that government provision of health insurance causes far more damage than any benefit it provides. The only intervention that might make sense, as part of an antipoverty program, is limited subsidies for the poor.

immigration

Rich countries around the world restrict immigration, a policy that receives widespread popular support. Advocates of restrictive policies rely on four possible arguments. First, that immigration dilutes existing languages, religions, family values, cultural norms, and so on. Second, that immigrants flock to countries with generous social welfare programs, leading to urban slums and inundated social networks. Third, that immigration can harm the sending country if the departing immigrants are high-skilled labor. Fourth, that immigration lowers the income of native, low-skill workers.

All of these arguments are wrong, overstated, or misguided. Immigration may change cultural values or norms, but nothing suggests this is a negative. Many societies flourish because they have incorporated new businesses, cultures, foods, and so on. More important, immigrants normally assimilate to the pre-existing culture provided government policy does not segregate them from the rest of society. In the past rich countries have incorporated large immigration flows with modest adjustment costs. Many of these immigrants lived in difficult conditions at first, but within a generation they achieved middle-class status or better.

The possibility that immigration puts pressure on the welfare state is a reasonable concern, although existing evidence does not suggest this is a major problem. In any case, the possibility that a generous social safety net might encourage immigration is a reason to moderate this safety net, rather than a reason to restrict immigration. Indeed, expanded immigration might create pressure to keep the welfare state modest.

The risk that immigration drains high-skilled labor from poor countries is real, but this kind of immigration has positive impacts on the sending country that mitigate against any negatives. The possibility of migration to a high-wage country generates an incentive to acquire education, and only some of those educated actually leave. The threat of a brain drain nudges poor countries away from bad policies—such as excessive tax rates—that generate the brain drain in the first place. Many immigrants send remittances to friends or relatives in their country of origin. Plus, if borders were really open, many immigrants would seek education abroad but return to their home country, knowing they could leave if economic factors so dictated. Similarly, with open borders many immigrants would pursue temporary stays in higher-wage countries. Temporary migration is common in many countries now and was common in the United States before the tightening of immigration rules in the 1910s and 1920s. Temporary migration raises fewer of the standard concerns than permanent migration, while still helping many people in low-wage countries.

Concern for the poor, assuming this includes the poor in other countries, argues for vastly expanded immigration since many potential immigrants are much poorer than the natives whose wages they might depress. Only a bizarre view of equity favors people earning the minimum wage in rich countries over people near starvation in developing countries.

The conclusion that open borders is the best immigration policy is all the stronger because attempts to restrict immigration have their own negatives. These include the direct costs of border controls, the creation of a violent black market for immigration, and incentives for corruption. Further, immigration may have beneficial effects on productivity by fostering competition and introducing new ideas, approaches, business models, products, and so on. At the same time, many people in receiving countries enjoy the influence of new cultures. Immigrants also work at jobs for which the native supply is small.

Reasonable people can argue that immigration should increase gradually to moderate the transition costs. But any reasonable balancing implies vastly expanded immigration relative to current levels. This would improve the welfare of poor people in other countries far more than **foreign aid**.

liberalism versus libertarianism

Liberalism used to be the term for the perspective now generally known as libertarianism. Over the 20th century, however, the term "liberal" has come to mean something radically different. Liberals—as the term is now understood—believe that markets and other private arrangements work poorly and that government intervention makes things better. Roughly, liberalism and libertarianism tend to overlap regarding social and foreign policy issues but not economic issues.

Liberals pay lip service to several underlying principles, such as the right to choice, the sanctity of life, and the value of helping the poor. Liberalism is nevertheless inconsistent in these and other dimensions. Liberals defend choice when it comes to abortion policy but not when it comes to parental decisions about parochial schools. Liberals argue for the sanctity of life when it comes to capital punishment but not when it comes to abortion. Liberals advocate for anti-poverty spending yet oppose expanded immigration.

The liberal desire for government intervention regarding a broad range of economic issues suggests that liberals do not believe people can make good choices on their own, and that government should intervene to improve those choices. Thus liberalism is at its essence a **paternalistic** position that assumes government knows better than the people being governed.

mandatory savings programs

Some people do not save enough for retirement and find themselves destitute in old age. One possible response is for governments to mandate that everyone save a certain fraction of their income.

Under a mandatory savings plan, employers withhold a percentage of each employee's wage or salary and place these amounts in stock or bond mutual funds. These personal accounts belong to the individual and earn a market rate of return. Starting at a government-specified retirement age, owners can withdraw their funds. Any amounts left in the accounts at death are part of the owner's bequeathable estate.

Mandatory savings programs sound like a promising way to reduce old-age poverty, but the reality is different.

The main problem is that mandatory savings programs do not necessarily raise savings; most households can undo the mandated savings by decreasing other savings. For example, those forced to save in a government program can save less in 401(k)s, IRAs, and similar plans, or take out bigger mortgages, car loans, and so on. Car dealers, real estate agents, and others who would like consumers to spend more are happy to explain to consumers how to undo mandated savings.

Mandatory savings policies do affect households that save less than the mandated amounts, especially low-income households that spend most of their income on food, clothing, shelter, and medical care. Increased saving is not obviously beneficial for a household that is barely making ends meet, however, since this delays access to money that might be better used sooner rather than later.

Most mandatory savings programs recognize that some people earn too little during their working years to accumulate reasonable retirement wealth, so they provide a minimum guaranteed level of income in addition to requiring a minimum savings rate. This means these programs are just income insurance for the elderly, and the mandatory savings component accomplishes nothing.

Beyond having small or even perverse effects, mandatory savings programs have unintended negatives. They distort retirement choices in the same way that **Social Security** does. The accumulations in mandatory savings accounts are tempting targets for taxation. The fact that government is implicitly promising a reasonable rate of return on mandated savings gives government an excuse to regulate financial markets. More broadly, mandatory savings programs endorse the view that people are too short-sighted or undisciplined to save for themselves. This is true for some people, but accepting a government role in such an important decision legitimizes a dangerous degree of **paternalism**.

A different incorrect argument for mandatory savings is that replacing Social Security with private accounts—mandatory savings by another name—would reduce the solvency problems faced by Social Security without reducing benefits or increasing taxes. This claim is wrong; see **private (personal) accounts**.

marriage and civil unions

In modern societies marriage is defined and regulated by government. When two persons enter a civil marriage, they acquire rights and responsibilities regarding division of property, inheritance, guardianship of children, and other issues. The government enforces these rights and responsibilities by adjudicating disputes. Thus civil marriage can be regarded as a bundle of contracts involving the marrying persons, their children, and others.

In most countries government provides marriage only to opposite-sex couples. Same-sex couples can enter private contracts that approximate some aspects of civil marriage, but they cannot legally marry. In other cases same-sex couples can enter civil unions, which mimic marriage in most respects but do not carry the same emotional significance.

Current practice raises two questions. The first is whether government should define and enforce the bundle of contracts known as marriage rather than enforcing private contracts that replicate components of marriage. The second is whether government should refer to this bundle as marriage and provide it only to opposite-sex couples.

In fact, government provision of marriage has no compelling justification; government can simply define and enforce default rules about each component.

A default rule about division of property could specify that all property belongs to the person who purchased it. A default rule about inheritance could specify that if a person writes a valid will, the government enforces it; otherwise, the property defaults to a charity. A default rule about guardianship could specify that the biological mother is a child's only legal parent unless the mother voluntarily gives up that status. This rule might also impose that the biological father is responsible for some percent of child support.

Under the private contracting approach, people could enter contracts that deviate from the default rules. A man and woman who wanted to live together could agree that all property is divided 50/50, and the government would enforce this contract. Couples could still enter religious marriages.

The private contracting approach avoids the polarization over whether marriage includes same-sex as well as opposite-sex couples. Opposite-sex couples and same-sex couples would have equal opportunity to live together, write wills, have biological or adopted children, and so on.

Some observers might nevertheless believe government marriage is superior to private contracting, perhaps at protecting children. No logical or empirical argument suggests that opposite-sex couples are better parents than same-sex couples, however, so if government supplies marriage, it should provide it to both same-sex and opposite-sex couples. Ideally government would call this civil union, to distinguish it from religious marriage.

medications

Drug manufacturers in most countries cannot sell their medications until they prove to regulators that the medicines are safe and efficacious. The argument for this regulation is that, unconstrained, manufacturers would sell drugs with limited efficacy or undisclosed side effects. Regulation may at times prevent faulty medicines from reaching the market, but overall such regulation is counterproductive.

Regulation forces drug development to be more costly and take longer than it would without regulation. Whether regulation is desirable, therefore, depends on how often it prevents unsafe or ineffective drugs versus how often it delays beneficial drugs and raises their costs. The likelihood is that the regulatory approach errs toward excessive caution.

To see why, consider the regulatory approval process. If regulators approve a drug that harms people, the public finds out and regulators face budget cuts or congressional hearings. If regulators test too much and induce delay, the cost is spread over lots of people, and no one notices. The bias in the regulatory approach is thus for too much testing because it's safer for the regulators. To give one example, the U.S. Food and Drug Administration long delayed the use of aspirin for heart attack patients, despite abundant clinical trials that showed the efficacy of this cheap, low-risk treatment.

This negative of regulation might be acceptable if the private sector could not hold drug manufacturers accountable in instances where a drug does not deliver as promised. In fact, two private mechanisms impose substantial discipline.

The first is competition between firms. A drug company that makes a faulty or ineffective product gets bad publicity and lower future sales. Companies thus try to develop reputations for quality products, and patients and doctors patronize these companies. Likewise, sensible patients and doctors exercise caution regarding new or unknown products.

The second private mechanism that promotes quality medicine is private organizations that conduct tests, certify quality, or maintain public databases with information about good and bad drugs (similar to *Consumer Reports*). Competition between these rating agencies makes them more efficient than a government regulator and allows a better balance between avoiding mistakes and delaying useful medicines.

Private rating agencies, moreover, could provide information about the risks and let different patients, along with their doctors, choose whether to try experimental drugs or ones with harsh side effects, rather than forcing one safety standard on everyone. In this way patients in more desperate circumstances, who are probably willing to take more risks, would have that option. Under current regulation drugs are usually either available or not, independent of the risks and regardless of the needs of particular patients.

The history of off-label prescribing in the United States provides evidence that private mechanisms are effective. Under

FDA rules, doctors can prescribe any approved drug for whatever conditions they wish, whether or not this was the originally intended use. Numerous drugs have found useful off-label applications, and the incidence of serious adverse effects has been rare.

Another alternative to regulation is **product liability**, which allows people harmed by drugs to sue manufacturers. This approach relies on private actions to initiate complaints but on the government to arbitrate and enforce any settlements. The risk of lawsuits encourages manufacturers to weigh the risks of selling a product too quickly against the lost profit of not selling it quickly enough. Nothing guarantees that each manufacturer gets it exactly right, but product liability at least gets incentives pointed in the right direction.

minimum legal drinking age

Most societies impose a minimum age for the purchase of alcohol. The presumed justification is that young people might easily fall prey to addiction if allowed to drink at too young an age, and they might impose harm on others such as by driving under the influence. Further, the standard reasoning goes, age restrictions do a reasonable job of preventing underage drinking.

A minimum legal drinking age is perhaps defensible in principle. Few people want to see 12-year-olds guzzling vodka or drunken 17-year-olds behind the wheel of a car. The value of minimum legal drinking ages is nevertheless unclear.

Teenagers routinely circumvent minimum drinking ages, so they learn that rules are made to be broken. Purveyors of alcohol who sell to underage customers gain at the expense of those who obey the law. Parents who assume age restrictions have addressed the problem of underage drinking may take less care to ensure the responsible behavior of their children.

Minimum legal drinking ages also appear to have only modest effects on underage drinking or related negatives such as traffic fatalities. Indeed, by glamorizing alcohol these laws may create a forbidden fruit and thereby encourage drinking. Relatedly, any diminished access to alcohol that results from minimum drinking ages might generate binge drinking if youths consume heavily when they do get access.

Thus, while mild age restrictions (such as 15 in many European countries) probably have small effects on youth alcohol use, good or bad, extreme age restrictions (such as 21 in the United States) probably do more harm than good.

minimum wages

Minimum-wage laws mandate that employers in covered sectors pay their employees at least a specified legal minimum wage per hour. In the United States, both the federal and state governments impose minimum wage laws. Historically these have not been especially high compared to the market wages for low-skill labor, but in some countries the minimum is well in excess of the wage that would prevail without the law.

Standard economics explains that a minimum wage reduces efficiency by artificially raising the price of low-skill labor. The only possible justification for a minimum wage, therefore, is a desire to raise the income of low-wage workers.

The minimum wage is a problematic policy for accomplishing this goal, however. The minimum wage reduces employment of low-skilled individuals, so it causes some people to have a zero wage even while it helps others have a higher wage. This effect appears to be modest in the United States because the legal minimum has not much exceeded the market wage of low-skilled labor. In other countries the effect is more substantial because the minimum wage is much higher relative to prevailing wages. In extreme cases the minimum wage causes employers to move factories overseas where wages are lower—thereby reducing employment opportunities in the home country—or to move their operations underground.

Even if the minimum wage has minor effects on low-skill employment, nothing ensures that minimum-wage jobs go to low-income adults rather than middle-class teenagers. The minimum wage also fuels the perception that employers cause low wages. In fact, employers who offer low wages for low-skill labor are doing exactly what economic efficiency dictates. The reason for low wages is low skill, which in turn reflects low education and training. Providing a higher wage when no training or education has occurred creates the wrong incentive for low-skill workers.

moral hazard

When people are insured against certain kinds of risks—that is, when they are protected against downside losses but get to keep any upside gains—their natural response may be to take more risks. This change in behavior that results from having insurance is known as moral hazard.

Many types of insurance generate moral hazard. Auto theft insurance causes car owners to be less vigilant about parking their cars in safe places (e.g., in a parking garage as opposed to on the street). Bicycle insurance encourages owners to buy less sturdy locks. Health insurance might cause people to demand more medical care and doctors to undertake more tests and procedures.

Moral hazard can also arise when the insurance is implicit rather than explicit. If governments are in the habit of bailing out businesses that take on excessive risk, then these businesses will take on more risk. This has been a crucial feature of banking history in the United States and elsewhere.

A number of government agencies create moral hazard by insuring private risk taking. The Federal Deposit Insurance Corporation insures bank deposits; the Pension Benefit Guarantee Corporation insures private pension funds; the Federal Housing Administration backstops mortgage loans. Each of these entities generates moral hazard by giving the relevant private parties a reduced incentive to worry about the risks of their decisions. For example, businesses whose pensions are guaranteed are likely to hold riskier assets in the pension portfolio. These risky assets earn more during good times, and if they fail the government covers some of the losses.

More broadly, government policies that attempt to eliminate fraud or prevent misleading business practices can also generate moral hazard. If investors believe the Securities and Exchange Commission has stopped unscrupulous companies from issuing stock, they may undertake less due diligence themselves. If consumers think the Consumer Product Safety Commission has banished faulty products, they may take less care to judge safety for themselves. If these policies are fully successful in banishing rogue companies or bad products from the marketplace, then the moral hazard induced is irrelevant. In practice, however, government attempts to discipline markets are imperfect, so the overly optimistic assurances provided by these policies can leave many consumers worse off.

morality

The consequential libertarian perspective on policy is often thought to leave no room for considerations of morality or social justice, but this concern is misplaced. Terms like "morality" and "justice" are just shorthand for consequences that are widely regarded as undesirable. For example, the view that war is immoral is really a consequential conclusion that war causes death and destruction without sufficient beneficial impacts to outweigh the negatives. Thus, morality and justice fit in the consequential framework, which simply makes explicit the consequences that underlie views about morality, justice, and similar values.

mutually beneficial exchange

A common negative of government policies is that they prevent mutually beneficial exchange (such interactions are referred to in economics as **Pareto efficient**). In some instances this is an unavoidable side effect, while in others it is the explicit goal of policy. Either way, and whether or not the policy serves a broader purpose, this effect is a cost of the policy.

Consider minimum wage laws as an example. These prevent employers from hiring employees at wages below the minimum. Some people, however, would rather work for low wages than not work at all. A minimum wage raises the income of some workers but only by preventing mutually beneficial interactions between employers and other workers. Therefore, not everyone is better off; those prevented from working get the short end of the stick, so minimum-wage laws are not Pareto efficient.

Much regulation has this characteristic. Occupational safety and health regulation prevents employers from hiring someone to do a risky job, even if that worker is aware of the risks and wishes to accept them. Collective bargaining laws prevent employers from hiring replacement workers who are willing to work at wages below union demands. Price controls keep consumers from voluntarily paying "excessive" prices. Antitrust laws prevent mergers between mutually agreeable companies. State regulations prevent insurance companies from offering policies that do not cover various medical conditions, such as fertility treatments. Child labor laws mean an ice cream store cannot hire a 13-year-old, even if the teenager and the parents agree this is a good use of that child's time. Prohibitions against gambling or the purchase and sale of drugs or sex prevent trades that both sides want to consummate.

The mere fact that a policy prevents mutually beneficial exchange is not by itself decisive. Such policies may achieve other goals. At a minimum, however, such policies are not unambiguously good, and any benefit they generate must be sufficient to offset the mutually beneficial trades they prevent. It is typically impossible to know if this is the case. Consider alcohol taxes as an example. Since these taxes harm responsible consumers, any benefits from reduced misuse of alcohol do not necessarily exceed the reduced enjoyment of alcohol by responsible users. Thus, regulation that prevents mutually beneficial exchange is immediately suspect.

In addition to policies that prevent voluntary exchange, many others mandate specific behavior that differs from what individuals or firms would choose voluntarily. These have the same negatives as policies that prevent mutually beneficial exchange, only in reverse. Compulsory education is a good example.

See also **children**.

national defense

One government policy that libertarians accept is provision of national defense, since no private solution is likely to prove satisfactory. A private group that attempted to field an army and defend the country would find it difficult to exclude any individual person from the benefits of this protection, since any activities that deterred potential attacks or warded off actual attacks would defend everyone within the country. Thus, most people would not voluntarily pay for national defense provided by a private group, so it is hard for such an activity to be profitable enough to induce adequate private provision. That is, national defense is what economists refer to as a public good.

The conclusion that government should provide some national defense applies to narrow self-defense activities, such as fielding an army that deters enemy attacks and responds to attacks that do occur. In practice, however, nations perform many inappropriate actions under the mantle of self-defense, most of them harmful.

One action that goes beyond strict self-defense is preemptive attacks on other countries, as in the U.S. invasion of Iraq. In rare instances preemptive strikes might be legitimate self-defense, and by moving first and preventing extended conflict, a government might save lives and property both at home and in the threatening country. A possible illustration is Israel's preemptive strike in 1967, when Egypt had troops massing at the Israeli border. In this case few doubted that the threat was imminent or that Egypt's intention was to harm Israel. The case for preemptive action was at least plausible.

In most instances of preemptive attack, however, the threat is not obvious, undeniable, or imminent. This justification for military action is therefore readily misused whenever leaders have other agendas but wish to hide behind the guise of self-defense. Thus, preemptive national defense deserves extreme suspicion, and most such actions are not wise uses of government resources. The U.S. invasion of Iraq is a textbook example.

Another problematic use of a country's self-defense capabilities is humanitarian or nation-building efforts that purport to help other countries. One objection to such actions might be that the helping country pays the costs while foreigners receive the benefits, but this is not the right criticism. The compassion argument for **redistributing income** holds that government should be willing to impose costs on society generally to raise the welfare of the least fortunate members. It is hard to see how this logic would apply only to people who are already residents of a given country.

The more persuasive criticism of humanitarian and nation-building efforts is that interventions that purport to help other countries have large costs to the helping country and tenuous benefits to the country being helped. The U.S. invasion and occupation of Iraq is again a good example. This intervention has been enormously costly to the United States, while the benefits to the Iraqi people are difficult to assess. On the plus side, the invasion removed a brutal dictator and established a nominally more democratic government. On the negative side, Iraqis experienced enormous loss of life and destruction of property during the invasion, and sectarian violence has continued. Any suppression of terrorism within Iraq has mainly shifted attacks to Afghanistan and Pakistan, so long-term stability in the region looks no better than before the invasion.

In practice, then, society rarely needs to balance the costs of humanitarian or nation- building activities against the benefits to the country being helped: Honest assessments usually suggest these benefits will be small. As with preemptive actions, therefore, the threshold for this kind of intervention should be incredibly high.

negative income tax

Anti-poverty programs in most economies are hodgepodges of multiple policies: cash transfers such as welfare payments, unemployment insurance, and disability insurance; in-kind transfers such as subsidized housing, free health insurance, and public schools; and sometimes voucher-style programs for education, housing, food, and the like.

A better approach is to replace all these programs with the negative income tax (NIT) advocated by Milton Friedman.

The NIT has two pieces: a minimum, guaranteed level of income, and a tax rate that is applied to any income earned. The net tax owed by any taxpayer depends on the gross tax liability—earned income times the tax rate—compared to the guaranteed minimum. If the gross liability exceeds the guaranteed minimum, the taxpayer owes the difference. If the gross liability falls short of the guaranteed minimum, the taxpayer receives the difference.

To illustrate, if the guaranteed minimum were $5,000 and the tax rate were 10 percent, a person earning no income would get a transfer from the government of $5,000 and have a total income of $5,000. A person earning $100,000 of income would have a gross tax liability of $10,000 and a net tax liability of $5,000, for a total, after-tax income of $95,000. A person earning $10,000 of income would have a gross liability of $1,000 and a net liability of negative $4,000 (that is, this person would get a check from the government for $4,000), for a total, after-tax income of $14,000.

The NIT is not perfect. It generates a disincentive to work because recipients keep only a fraction of each dollar earned. But the distorting effects of the NIT are likely to be less than those of current welfare systems because these often incorporate much higher (implicit) tax rates on income. That is, the hodgepodge of existing transfer programs sometimes takes away so much in benefits when a recipient's income increases that the recipient is only slightly better off, or, in a few cases, worse off. Recipients then face minimal incentive to earn extra income or reduce their reliance on government support.

The NIT has further advantages over current approaches. The rules are clear, so taxpayers waste less time and money complying with the tax code. One government agency (presumably the same one that collects the income tax) can implement this policy. The NIT does not distort particular markets as occurs with in-kind transfers, nor does it create political controversy over issues such as whether Medicaid should fund abortions. The amount of income being transferred is easy to understand in comparison to systems where one must aggregate over multiple programs, convert in-kind transfers to cash equivalents, and so on, to gauge the overall magnitude of redistribution. The amount of redistribution should be clear so that society can honestly debate the appropriate level.

nuclear power

One major environmental controversy is whether government should allow or promote nuclear power. Environmentalists traditionally oppose nuclear power because of the risk of a major catastrophe and the costs of disposing of nuclear waste. Advocates of nuclear power see these concerns as exaggerated; they claim that the costs of nuclear power are low relative to alternative energy sources, that use of nuclear power reduces reliance on foreign oil, and that avoiding the use of fossil fuel alleviates global warming. It might seem hard to sort out these claims, especially since one cost, the risk of a nuclear accident, is horrific but rare.

In fact, the problem with nuclear power is that government intervention makes the costs appear artificially low, which gives private markets excessive incentive to invest in this energy source. In the United States, the Price-Anderson Act of 1957 limits the liability of the nuclear power industry in the case of accidents. In other countries governments own and operate the nuclear industry and, implicitly, insure themselves, thereby hiding the liability cost of nuclear power. The provision of free insurance is crucial, since the potential for a horrific event, while small, is not zero. Without government-subsidized insurance, the nuclear power industry would have to buy private insurance, which would be prohibitively expensive. Thus the true costs of nuclear power are much higher than they appear, and the private sector might stop investing in nuclear power if the government just stopped subsidizing it.

organ sales

The sale of human body parts is banned in most societies, but this prohibition makes little sense. As long as these are voluntary, the exchange makes both parties better off. In the case of kidneys, donors can profit directly by selling one kidney while functioning normally on the remaining one. In the case of other organs, potential donors can raise money for their family and friends by selling the rights to their organs upon death. These transactions have enormous potential to help people with serious diseases that can be ameliorated with an organ transplant.

The principal objection to organ sales holds that short-sighted or desperate individuals would be lured by large monetary rewards into selling organs against their own interests. This concern is understandable but oversold. Doctors and hospitals, along with family and friends, would prevent most such abuses. Informed consent rules would alert potential organ sellers to the risks they faced. Further, even modest payments for organs from deceased donors are likely to generate such a large increase in the supply that prices for these organs would be modest and thus not a major inducement to short-sighted behavior.

Even if organ sales are not fully legal, monetary mechanisms could expand the supply in ways that should not raise major concerns about the rationality of donor behavior. If a private business were allowed to offer small monetary inducements to potential donors to get them to register, and then sell this information to hospitals, the potential supply would likely expand significantly. Some people register as organ donors now when they get a driver's license, but many neglect this option. Most, however, would be happy to register for, say, $100.

Pareto efficiency

See **mutually beneficial exchange.**

partial-birth abortion

The so-called partial-birth **abortion** is normally used in late-term abortions and involves delivering a fetus except for the head, puncturing the fetus's skull inside the womb, removing the fetus's brain, and then extracting the remaining fetus. Everyone finds this procedure unappealing, or worse, so support for banning the procedure is widespread, even among many who support legal abortion.

Banning partial-birth abortion, however, does little to reduce late-term abortions because other methods for late-term abortion exist. A ban also harms some women by affecting the way such abortions occur. A federal ban is especially bad because it inserts the federal government in an issue appropriately left to the states.

Thus a ban on partial-birth abortion is a feel-good policy that allows politicians to cater to pro-life interest groups while not actually reducing abortion and perhaps even harming some women.

paternalism

A standard justification for government policies is the claim that many individuals make bad decisions when left to their own devices: People may be short-sighted, ill-informed, undisciplined, or in some way not rational. Thus, according to the paternalists, governments can make such people better off by encouraging or requiring different choices than these people would make on their own. This reasoning is at the heart of policies like **mandatory savings programs**, **consumer protection laws**, bans against vice, compulsory education laws, warning labels on food and medicine, and more.

No one denies that some individuals are not fully rational and do not seem to act in their own self-interest. Many individuals are rational, of course, and private mechanisms like competition provide substantial protections for those who are not. Nevertheless, it might seem plausible that in some cases government can protect people from themselves. The paternalistic defense of intervention, however, is problematic.

To begin, the question for policy is not whether irrationality exists but whether interventions that target this irrationality do more good than harm. This is possible but hardly guaranteed, since interventions have their own costs (see **drug prohibition**, **false or misleading advertising**, and **consumer protection policies**). One major obstacle is that policies that protect the irrational from themselves inevitably harm the rational. A **sin tax** on alcohol, for example, might discourage drinking by people who abuse alcohol, but it also raises the cost for responsible drinkers.

A second reason for caution is that paternalism can seem to justify an enormous range of government intervention (see **slippery slopes**). Paternalism might suggest, for example, that government should discourage not only drug use or insufficient savings, but also saturated fat, lack of exercise, excessive television, certain books, and particular religious preferences. In each case a plausible argument exists that some people consume the wrong amount of the good in question, yet most people would be wary of intervention that dictates religious choices, dietary restrictions, or a jogging regimen. More broadly, paternalism opens the door for interventions that would horrify those who invoke paternalism in other contexts. Paternalism might suggest, for example, banning abortion because most women prevented from obtaining an abortion nevertheless end up loving their kids.

Even without slippery slopes, government attempts to prevent every bad decision would consume enormous resources. Thus politics and prejudice can play a large role in determining which goods come in for paternalistic considerations. Marijuana use, for example, carries health risks, but even long-term, heavy use appears to generate less harm than being obese.

These concerns do not prove that paternalism is always un-warranted. Policies that seek to protect children, for example, are relatively defensible both because children are more likely to make poor decisions and because bad decisions that parents make on behalf of their children seem more troubling than those parents make for themselves. Even in these cases, how-ever, slippery slopes can cause plausibly defensible paternal-ism (a **minimum legal drinking age** of 16) to evolve into excessive paternalism (a minimum legal drinking age of 21).

personal income taxation

The tax systems in most economies focus substantially on per-sonal income taxation. This means that the tax base consists of the wages, salaries, bonuses, dividends, interest, capital gains, and other payments received by individuals. Personal income taxation is not necessarily the ideal tax system (see **consump-tion taxes**), but since many economies employ income taxa-tion, it is useful to ask what structure a reasonable system should have.

A first desirable feature is the absence of exemptions, de-ductions, credits, or other special treatment of different kinds of income. These aspects of existing income tax systems do not usually have a convincing justification. Even when they do, they complicate the tax system, encourage wasteful avoidance behavior, and open the tax system to political manipulation.

Consider the deductibility of charitable contributions. De-ductibility plausibly increases charitable giving beyond what would otherwise occur. The problem is that deductibility means government must define what constitutes a religion or what should be considered educational. This privileges established religions or educational perspectives; more generally, it entrenches the status quo. Related problems arise with respect to many special features of the tax code, such as the deductibility of mortgage interest or tax credits for clean energy.

Favored tax treatment of a few activities might have a plausible justification; for example, tuition tax credits might be a reasonable way to subsidize education. Policy can instead accomplish this goal through education vouchers, however, which keeps the tax code simple and enhances compliance and enforcement.

The ideal rate structure for an income tax is less clear, but a natural base case is a **flat tax**—a system with one rate that applies to every dollar of income, regardless of the amount of income earned.

This approach has the virtue of simplicity, and it avoids a range of distortions that arise in real-world tax systems (for example, this system has no marriage penalty). Hardly anyone advocates a pure flat tax, however, presumably because it requires people with low incomes to pay positive amounts in taxes. A second possibility, therefore, is to incorporate a **negative income tax**. A system with this structure can accomplish the reasonable distributional goal of alleviating poverty without imposing progressive income tax rates.

Nothing proves that a flat tax is superior to a system with more rates. Likewise, nothing dictates that any specific degree of progressivity is the right amount. But **redistribution** among middle- and higher-income taxpayers is not compelling, so distributional considerations do not make a strong case for more rates. In addition, pragmatic considerations argue for the simplicity of a flat tax. With only one tax rate, taxpayers know readily their after-tax return from work and savings. With everyone paying taxes, no one can assume that additional government expenditure is free.

philosophical libertarianism

See also **consequential versus philosophical libertarianism.**

polarization

An important negative of many government policies is that they can breed a polarized, embittered society. This occurs because people have to obey policies they dislike or see their tax dollars used for activities they believe to be offensive or wasteful.

A good illustration is *Roe v. Wade*, the Supreme Court's 1973 decision that barred states from banning **abortion**. This created a level of anger among abortion opponents that would have been avoided if abortion policy had been left to the states, even if many states had gradually liberalized abortion access (as was occurring in the early 1970s). This does not necessarily make the court's decision incorrect, but it is one cost of that approach.

A different example is public schools, which by their nature must take stands on issues such as affirmative action, prayer, dress and speech codes, curricular content, teaching methods, and more. To take one particular case, some parents are strong advocates of school prayer, while others are ardent opponents. Public schools have no room for compromise on this issue; they must accept the ban dictated by the Supreme Court's interpretation of the First Amendment. Private schools can require prayer, or offer prayer without compelling all students to participate, or avoid prayer entirely, as they see fit. Parents then choose a school whose policy they can accept, balanced against other positives or negatives of that school.

Similar examples abound. Because it is in the marriage business, government must take a stand on what constitutes a marriage and therefore be either for or against gay marriage. Because it funds science, government must take a stand on whether to support stem cell research. Because it funds the arts, government must decide whether work that some find profound but others find offensive is actually art. Because it funds TV and radio, government implicitly supports some opinions over others, breeding resentment from those who disagree with the views expressed.

The fact that policies have a tendency to polarize is one reason to keep intervention at the state rather than the federal level. This allows variety, which softens the hard feelings generated by federal imposition of one policy on everyone. Even residents of a state who do not like their own state's policy can take some comfort in the possibility of moving to another state or even in the existence of a more preferred policy elsewhere.

private (personal) accounts

An issue that confronts many economies is the apparent insolvency of their Social Security programs. As currently operated in the United States and other countries, these programs levy specific Social Security taxes that flow into a Social Security Trust Fund, and the programs pay benefits out of this fund. The inflow does not necessarily match the outflow, since program parameters and economic conditions affect both tax revenues and benefit payments. In particular, changes in the number of working-age versus retired persons can substantially change the financial condition of such funds. Thus current projections indicate the U.S. and other trust funds will hit zero within a few decades. These pending imbalances are viewed by many as a problem, and they generate a demand to fix Social Security programs.

Conservative and some libertarian groups have suggested restoring balance by introducing **mandatory savings programs**, which are euphemistically described as "personal accounts" (or as "privatization" of Social Security). The idea is this: Rather than having Social Security taxes go into the Trust Fund, some or all of these revenues would go into accounts identified with the individual contributor. Each participant would invest these amounts in stock or bond mutual funds, and the contributions and accumulated returns would be one source of retirement income.

The assumption behind this approach is that personal accounts would earn a higher return than Social Security. In particular, the return on Social Security contributions—the benefits received relative to taxes paid—is only 2 to 3 percent, while the return on stocks has historically been about 7 percent. Thus, letting people save via personal accounts appears to increase the return on savings and therefore reduce Trust Fund imbalance.

Personal accounts accomplish little, however, because creation of these accounts does not change the benefits promised to current and future Social Security beneficiaries. Thus, assuming policy honors these commitments, the decrease in Social Security tax revenue caused by creation of personal accounts must be accompanied by an increase in other taxes. That means the after-tax income of households does not change, so savings does not change. Instead, the increased savings in personal accounts is offset by decreased savings elsewhere. Thus the stock market rate of return is irrelevant; it is a higher return on a zero increase in savings.

Using personal accounts to increase solvency is therefore a mirage; improving solvency can only occur via increased taxation or reduced benefits.

product liability

Under the laws of many countries, businesses that sell defective products are liable for any damages these products might cause. A company that sells a defective toaster oven, for example, can be forced to repay its cost and to compensate the buyer for any harm done, such as a fire the toaster oven started. These laws mean that sellers of faulty products should not expect a significant or long-term financial gain from products that do not perform as advertised or that generate accidents or injury from normal use. If the product liability system works smoothly, the sellers end up gaining little from faulty products or services.

Product liability systems do not work perfectly. Sometimes they fail to deter unscrupulous sellers; other times they impose unreasonably large awards (e.g., $2 million because a hot cup of coffee from a fast food chain, opened while the buyer was driving a car, spilled and burned her).

Despite these imperfections, product liability provides a useful constraint on firms by reducing the incentive to sell products that do not work as advertised or that cause significant harm. The existence of product liability is one reason consumer protection policies are unnecessary.

The main advantage of product liability is that it imposes few costs on businesses that behave responsibly. It is also less easily politicized than regulation, and because bringing suits is costly, the system tends to focus on significant harms, not trivial ones. A product liability system gives consumers the incentive to monitor firm behavior, and this is broader and more consistent than any monitoring done by a few bureaucrats. Relying on product liability also avoids sending the false signal that a government regulatory body has eliminated faulty products.

Attempts at reform of the product liability system have focused on limiting punitive damages awards—those imposed on top of any compensation for actual damages—because punitives sometimes seem excessive. It is not obvious that legal limits matter in practice, however, since juries can just inflate the compensatory damages to offset any limits on punitives.

professional licensure

One kind of regulation imposed in many industries is professional licensure that requires individuals in certain occupations to acquire specific training and pass particular tests before offering their services in the marketplace. Current licensure applies to lawyers, doctors, nurses, plumbers, hair stylists, and more. To understand the effects of this licensure, consider doctors.

To practice medicine legally, physicians must have graduated from an accredited medical school, passed an examination, and received a license to practice medicine from a state licensing board. The standard argument for licensing is that it protects patients from incompetent or unscrupulous doctors. A related argument is that many consumers are not sufficiently informed to choose a reasonable-quality doctor.

Even if licensing increases the average quality of doctors, it reduces the quantity by restricting entry into this profession, with the result that consumers face higher prices for medical care. Absent the legal restrictions, a broader range of people with less or faster training could provide much health care that does not require the advanced knowledge of a fully trained doctor. Nurses or physicians assistants, for example, could provide basic checkups, preventive medicine, and many routine procedures. This already occurs to a substantial degree, but the scope for such cost saving is far greater than current regulation permits. The net effect of licensing doctors may therefore be to reduce the health of the population rather than increase it.

Licensure is also unnecessary because mechanisms such as reputation and malpractice liability can discipline incompetent or unethical doctors without the need for government restrictions on becoming a doctor. Consumers who are not well informed can purchase health care from established HMOs.

Existing licensure rules do not eliminate low-quality doctors in any case but instead create barriers to competition from qualified physicians. In particular, these rules make it difficult for foreign-trained doctors to work in the United States even when their qualifications are similar to, or better than, those of U.S.-trained doctors.

The case for licensing doctors is therefore weak, and these same considerations apply to licensure generally. Indeed, the case against licensure is even stronger for many other professions (e.g., plumbers, hair stylists) because consumers can better judge quality for themselves and because the costs of choosing a bad supplier are less severe.

property rights

One version of the libertarian perspective states that the only legitimate government interventions are those that define and enforce property rights. Thus national defense is an appropriate activity of government under this libertarian view because it protects the property of a country's residents against theft by outsiders. Likewise, criminal justice activities are desirable because they protect the property of one person from being taken inappropriately by another. In contrast, virtually all other interventions are unacceptable because they violate property rights. Redistributing income takes property from one person to give it to another. A minimum-wage law prevents an employer from using his property—the business—in the most profitable manner. Outlawing prostitution prevents women from selling the use of their property—their bodies—in whatever manner they choose.

What this perspective fails to explain is why certain property rights are the ones that governments should protect. While some specifics are not especially subtle or controversial (most people agree that an individual has a right to personal belongings like clothing or a car), many are much more contentious (such as what rights an individual has over his or her own body, whether for organ sales, prostitution, or drug use). Thus, arguments over one policy versus another can readily be framed as the question of which property rights should be enforced by government, but adopting this framework does not by itself resolve the debates.

prostitution

In the United States prostitution has been illegal in most areas since the early decades of the 20th century. Prostitution is legal in some parts of Nevada and in Rhode Island, as well as in many other countries.

Opponents of prostitution argue that it is immoral, or that it breeds crime and violence, or that it spreads disease. In fact, it is outlawing prostitution that generates these outcomes, not prostitution itself. As with other vices, prohibition drives the market underground, so disagreements between prostitutes, johns, and pimps get resolved with violence rather than lawsuits. In places where prostitution is legal, the incidence of violence is far lower. A legal industry, moreover, is more likely to compete on the basis of quality, specifically, prostitutes who are tested for sexually transmitted diseases (STDs).

See also **drug prohibition.**

public health campaigns

One way that governments attempt to promote good health is through educational campaigns that encourage nutrition and exercise, and that discourage allegedly unhealthy behaviors like smoking or drinking. Providing the public with information might seem like a no-brainer, but these programs have serious negatives.

No one knows what diet or exercise regime is ideal, and the path to good health is not the same for everyone. Government health messages can therefore push everyone toward something that is far from perfect or even counterproductive (e.g., government nutritional guidelines from the 1930s that suggested a serving of eggs each day). In other instances, government health messages are so extreme that they reduce the credibility of all such messages (e.g., anti-drug ads like "This is your brain on drugs").

Beyond these limitations, few public health campaigns have been found to influence behavior in the desired directions. A plethora of anti-drug campaigns, for example, have yielded negligible or perverse effects on the frequency of drug use. And these campaigns are expensive, so it is difficult to argue they generate benefits in excess of costs.

public schools

The most common way that governments **subsidize education** is by owning and operating public schools that supply education at below-market prices. For K–12 public schools, the price faced by consumers is usually zero. For government colleges and universities, the price is zero or well below the market level at comparable private institutions.

Even if the arguments for subsidizing education are convincing, they do not mean that governments should operate schools. The arguments for subsidy merely suggest that governments should make the price of education lower than it would be if government did not subsidize. If, for example, some parents cannot afford education for their children, then a policy that provides these parents with additional purchasing power allows them to pay for private school and obviates the need for public schools.

The most obvious way to lower the price parents face for education is to provide **vouchers**, pieces of paper that parents can use to pay for private schools. These institutions accept the vouchers as payment because the government promises to redeem them for cash. Vouchers do not resolve all possible controversies regarding education, but they foster competition in the education market and thereby promote better educational outcomes and lower costs than public schools. This occurs in part because competition drives private schools to innovate, and in part because private schools are typically free of regulations imposed on public schools, such as policies requiring unionized teachers.

Another advantage of vouchers over public schools is that government involvement is less direct, which reduces the controversy associated with numerous issues that arise in subsidizing education. Consider religious schools as an example. It would almost certainly be unconstitutional and against accepted norms for government in the United States to operate parochial schools. It is probably not unconstitutional or against social norms, however, for government to provide education vouchers that parents can choose to spend on a parochial school. Thus the voucher approach, while not eliminating controversy, provides a mechanism for reasonable compromise.

public television and radio

The U.S. and other governments provide significant funding for television and radio stations that compete in the market with private providers. The argument for such funding is that certain kinds of "good programming" would not survive in the marketplace without such subsidies. This might be true, but it does not justify subsidies.

The problem with subsidies is that they put the government in the position of deciding what constitutes good programming. In mild cases such government decision making seems innocuous; no great harm is done if PBS shows more episodes of *Masterpiece Theater* than paying customers would choose on their own. When government-supported media produce news and information, however, the scope for subtle and not-so-subtle forms of thought control becomes substantial.

The political perspective of National Public Radio in the United States, for example, is unquestionably liberal rather than conservative. Since taxpayer dollars are involved, this is utterly inappropriate. The fact that subsidies occur is also **polarizing**. Those who disagree with NPR's perspective do not just change the station; they also resent the fact that their money is promoting views they do not share and may even find offensive.

In any event, the claim that various kinds of "desirable" programming cannot survive in the marketplace does not appear to be factually correct in most cases. Commercial stations regularly carry both entertainment and news programs that are barely distinguishable from those on public television and radio (e.g., the History Channel, A&E, *20/20*). No doubt some programming would appear less often due to lack of market demand, but this does not justify taking money from taxpayers generally to benefit those with particular tastes.

recycling

One popular environmental policy is the mandated recycling of residential waste products, such as newspapers, glass bottles, and plastic containers. Many local governments require or provide curbside pickup of recyclables in addition to collecting household trash, or they accept voluntary drop-off of recyclables at town dumps and other locations.

Proponents of government recycling programs rely on one or more of four arguments. First, that dumping trash in a landfill generates externalities such as contamination of groundwater. Second, that recycling reduces pollution by avoiding the production of new goods. Third, that recycling prevents depletion of the natural resources used to make such goods. Fourth, that reducing trash prevents exhaustion of landfill space. All these claims are wrong or misguided.

Most landfills are not toxic waste sites full of hazardous commercial by-products; they contain residential garbage, and they are generally non-toxic and safe. Parks, golf courses, and shopping centers routinely locate on landfills that have been closed and covered. Thus, assuming reasonable precautions, landfills do not endanger water supplies, cause disease, or even create long-term eyesores.

The second argument for recycling—that it reduces pollution associated with production of new goods—is weak and possibly even backwards. Production of many goods generates pollution, but so does recycling. Collecting, hauling, and sorting recyclables causes air pollution from the emissions generated by energy use. Cleaning newsprint or plastic so that it can be recycled requires toxic chemicals that pollute water supplies. The net pollution from recycling can therefore be only slightly less than—or even greater than—the pollution from producing new goods.

The third argument—that recycling conserves natural resources used in the production of new goods—is also misplaced, whether for renewable resources like trees or exhaustible resources like oil. As the supply of a given resource declines, its price rises. This encourages consumers and firms to substitute toward other goods. Further, higher prices generate additional exploration for new supplies and spur innovation that facilitates conservation of the resource.

For all these reasons, the prices of raw materials show, if anything, downward trends over time, the opposite of what should occur if these resources were becoming more scarce. Even if the supply of a particular commodity is declining, this does not mean society is using it excessively. In fact, it makes sense to use up exhaustible resources eventually because holding them in reserve forever benefits no one. The right question is therefore at what rate to draw down stocks of a nonrenewable resource. Private markets, it turns out, provide the appropriate incentives because prices for exhaustible resources rise as they become scarcer.

The concern over landfill space is similarly misguided. Even if landfill sites cannot be used for other purposes once closed, the area available for landfill is huge relative to the garbage the entire world can generate over a long time period. For example, a landfill roughly ten miles square could accommodate all of America's trash for the next one hundred years.

The reason many landfills are near capacity is not that suitable space is running out but that excess capacity is costly. Thus landfill operators do not open new sites until existing ones are close to filling up. Plus, the same reasoning applies here as for any exhaustible resource: The fact that it is in finite supply does not mean society is using it too quickly. As space for landfill becomes scarce, the cost of dumping trash at landfills will increase. This generates an incentive for consumers to produce less waste and for businesses to develop packaging that generates less trash.

The arguments in favor of recycling thus do little to suggest that recycling has a significant environmental benefit. The right question, moreover, is not just what environmental impact recycling has but whether any benefit in this direction is worth the cost. Residential recycling is far more expensive than hauling trash to a landfill, so the net impact of such policies is negative for any plausible estimate of the environmental benefit.

Government-mandated or subsidized recycling is therefore difficult to justify, although this difficulty is separate from whether private recycling makes sense. It does for some products, and private markets have recycled for centuries without government pressure or subsidy (e.g., the sale of used auto parts from junkyards). This occurs when the private costs of recycling are less than the private costs of producing new goods—the right condition unless producing new goods produces far more pollution, relative to the private costs, than does producing goods via recycling. The evidence, however, shows that any reductions in pollution from recycling are small on net, so it is implausible that these reductions could justify the large direct costs of mandated recycling programs.

redistributing income

Governments attempt to redistribute income in three main ways. The first is **anti-poverty programs** such as welfare, food stamps, Medicaid, or a **negative income tax**. The second is progressive income taxation, a system in which the amount of tax owed increases relative to income as the level of income increases. The third is policies that intervene in markets for specific goods and services, such as **minimum-wage laws**, **union** protections, regulatory limits on peak-load pricing, rent controls, price caps on medicines, anti–sweat shop laws, **agricultural subsidies**, anti–price-gouging laws, anti-scalper laws, anti-usury laws, and more.

Anti-poverty spending is the most defensible kind of redistribution. The goal of this redistribution—helping the poor—is reasonable, and the costs of a well-designed, limited anti-poverty program (e.g., a **negative income tax** set on a state-by-state basis) are modest.

Progressive income taxation is much harder to defend. The standard arguments for progressive taxation are the same as those for anti-poverty programs (compassion, social insurance), but these are far less convincing when applied to redistribution for the non-poor. Differences in income among the non-poor reflect numerous factors that people choose, such as education, effort, risk taking, and leisure. Likewise, households in the middle and upper part of the income distribution have far more opportunities than the poor to insure against job loss or adverse health events via savings, working spouses, and so on.

The costs of redistribution are also much greater at higher levels of income. Taxation distorts saving and labor-supply decisions to a greater degree because higher-income households have more opportunity to substitute away from work, such as by having one spouse withdraw from the labor force, or by channeling their saving to tax-preferred investments. The intangible negatives of redistribution, like creating the norm that low income is someone else's fault, are stronger as well.

Thus the general redistribution among the non-poor that progressive income taxation aims to achieve has no convincing justification and substantial costs. No obvious dividing line exists between redistribution to alleviate poverty and general redistribution. Policy can nevertheless recognize this distinction and avoid policies like progressive taxation that do not have a firm basis in alleviating poverty.

Redistribution via intervention in specific markets is rarely desirable. As a rule such policies distort economic incentives with at best ambiguous effects on the distribution of income. Thus if a society wishes to redistribute, it should do so explicitly via income transfers, not by interfering in specific markets.

religion

The prevailing view in the United States and many countries is that governments should be neutral about religion. The first amendment to the U.S. Constitution, for example, states that "Congress shall make no law respecting an establishment of religion, or prohibiting the free exercise thereof; . . ."

In fact, U.S. policy is decidedly pro-religion. First, the tax code designates religious institutions as nonprofit enterprises and therefore imposes no tax on their revenues (collections, membership fees, bake sale proceeds, and so on). Second, contributions to religious institutions (and other charitable activities) are tax deductible. Third, most religious institutions are exempt from property taxation imposed by local governments. All these special provisions subsidize religious institutions (and other nonprofits or charities) relative to for-profit activities and non-charities.

Making policy neutral toward religion would therefore require several changes in current tax codes. Fortuitously, the ideal changes are desirable independent of religion.

The main required modification is elimination of taxes on business income like the **corporate income tax**. Taxation of business income requires governments to define what constitutes a business, which then creates the opportunity to treat some as for-profit and some as nonprofit. If instead the system recognized that all income accrues to people, and only taxed wages, salaries, dividends, capital gains, and so on, the distinction between profit and nonprofit businesses would never arise. Taxation of business income is undesirable in part because it gets government involved in inappropriate issues, such as defining religion, but also because it fosters the perception that taxes are free because they can be imposed on businesses rather than people. This is false, since all businesses are owned by people.

To prevent the subsidy for religion that arises from the deductibility of charitable contributions, tax codes can eliminate this feature (ideally along with all other deductions and exemptions). As discussed under **personal income taxation**, an income tax system without any deductions or exemptions is likely more efficient than one that treats different kinds of income differently.

Once the tax code has stopped defining for-profit versus not-for-profit activity, and stopped designating some activities as charities, it is straightforward for local governments to impose the same property tax rate on all property. This is again desirable independent of the desire to make policy neutral toward religion: It keeps the tax code neutral about the different possible uses of property.

Libertarians are not for or against religion; they oppose government policies that favor religion, in part because this means government must define what constitutes a religion. This will inevitably favor the status quo at the expense of smaller, newer religions, and at the expense of individual liberty.

Roe v. Wade

In the United States, much of the debate over **abortion** centers on the Supreme Court's 1973 *Roe v. Wade* decision, which holds that the federal constitution bars states from banning abortion. Advocates of legal abortion defend *Roe* as both correct and essential to the continued legality of abortion, while opponents see *Roe* as mistaken and look to reverse it as a first step in reducing or eliminating legal abortion.

To understand the controversy, it is necessary to review the history of abortion policy in the United States. As of 1960, abortion was illegal under state law in every state, but federal law was silent on abortion. This situation began to change during the 1960s, when several states legalized abortion under circumstances such as rape, incest, or to protect the health of the mother. Starting in 1970, several states eliminated all legal restrictions on abortion, and in 1973 the U.S. Supreme Court ruled in *Roe v. Wade* that the U.S. Constitution bars states from banning abortion.

Because of *Roe*, abortion has been legal in all states since 1973. But *Roe* left the door open for state regulation of second- and third-trimester abortions, and many states impose some restrictions, including parental notification rules, post-viability bans, waiting periods, spousal consent laws, and licensed physician rules. In addition, some states and the federal government have banned a procedure called **partial-birth abortion**.

If it were indisputable that legal abortion is the right policy, it might seem natural to impose this policy at the federal level. Otherwise, some states might adopt a different policy, with adverse consequences to the residents of that state. Indeed, both liberals and conservatives frequently want the federal government to impose one abortion policy on all states, even while holding opposite views on what that policy should be.

The choice between state and federal policy, however, depends on more than choosing the perfect policy. Abortion is an emotional topic in an inherently gray area. Imposing one view

polarizes society and ignores the fact that divergent but defensible views exist. A reasonable approach, therefore, is to overturn *Roe* and leave abortion policy to the states. This does not mean banning abortion; instead, it restores the pre-1973 situation in which states rather than the federal government choose how to regulate abortion. This would be consistent with the fact that states regulate murder, and defining legal abortion is logically part of defining murder.

Under this approach, abortion would be widely available. Many states would allow legal abortion with few restrictions. Some states would allow legal abortion, but with more restrictions, while a few states might ban abortion entirely. Overall, most women would have access to legal, early term abortions and usually mid- and late-term abortions as well.

This is exactly what was occurring in the United States before the *Roe* decision. Five states, including California and New York, had already legalized. Roughly a dozen other states had legalized in cases of rape, incest, and to protect the health of the mother. In some instances this last exception was interpreted broadly to include the mother's mental health and future condition. Moreover, the rate of legal abortion was substantial and growing in states that had not legalized, because residents crossed into legalized-abortion states.

The outcome in which some states allow abortion on demand, while others impose some restrictions or ban abortion entirely, is not ideal from the perspective of those who oppose all restrictions. But a state-by-state approach is consistent with the views of a broad majority of the population, since many people do not view unrestricted abortion access as the only acceptable policy. The state-by-state approach therefore avoids the polarization created by forcing one policy on every-one. It is also a more plausible interpretation of the Constitu-tion, which does not explicitly or convincingly protect a right to abortion.

More broadly, overturning *Roe* and leaving states free to choose abortion policy would accept the unavoidable tradeoffs involved in regulating abortion. Given this ambiguity and the potential for controversy, it is good for policy to be less rather than more centralized. This approach may not be perfect, but it is plausibly the best society can do. It is also consistent with the libertarian perspective that leaving policy to state govern-ments is beneficial in most cases.

The legal status of abortion in other countries is consistent with the analysis here. In many countries the laws are interme-diate between the highly restrictive laws that existed in the United States before 1960 and the far less restrictive laws that exist now.

See also **federalism.**

RU-486

An interesting aspect of the **abortion** controversy is RU-486, more commonly known as the abortion or morning-after pill, a drug taken early in pregnancy that induces a medical rather than a surgical abortion. RU-486 has been used in Europe since 1989, but the U.S. Food and Drug Administration (FDA) did not approve it until 2000. The demand for RU-486 would plausibly have been stronger if *Roe v. Wade* had not mandated legal abortion in all states.

The availability of RU-486 may gradually defuse the abortion debate. The drug can be taken early in pregnancy, so it does not generate concerns about late-term abortions. RU-486 is administered orally in the privacy of a physician's office, and it requires no surgery or other invasive procedures. This means that if most women obtain abortions via RU-486, clinics that abortion opponents can bomb or protest will become rare. RU-486 can also be supplied in rural areas, small towns, and states that restrict abortion.

The RU-486 story provides a cautionary tale regarding liberal enthusiasm for regulation. Most liberals support regulation of the production and marketing of new medicines, such as that carried out in the United States by the Food and Drug Administration. As argued under **medications**, however, the FDA has unintended consequences, and the RU-486 history illustrates these perfectly. Had the FDA never existed, millions of women would have had earlier, legal access to abortion independent of *Roe*.

saving for retirement

See **Social Security** *and* **mandatory savings programs**.

self-reliance

A serious side effect of the broad range of government policies employed in modern economies is that it sends the message that people are too naïve or ill-informed to make reasonable decisions on their own. Some people may benefit from being protected from themselves (see **paternalism**), but policies that attempt this can reduce self-reliance and be counterproductive.

Bans on **false or misleading advertising** are one example, since they give people an excuse not to worry about the claims businesses make for their products. Government enforcement of a ban can never be significant without an extraordinary investment of enforcement resources. So, questionable claims occur despite the government ban. Unless people use common sense, therefore, they can easily be misled despite existing law. Numerous other policies reduce self-reliance: prohibitions on drugs, nutritional guidelines, regulation of decency content on television, safety regulation, food labeling laws, and licensure restrictions for doctors and lawyers.

Government intervention therefore promotes the false message that people do not need to think for themselves because the government has taken care of it. No matter how large government becomes, however, it cannot be everywhere or make every decision. Likewise, decisions have different consequences for different people. Unless people use common sense, or rely on private institutions that provide useful guidelines, they will make many bad decisions or be taken advantage of in many situations.

sin taxes

Many societies regard certain goods or activities as sinful, and a common policy response is sin taxation, meaning a tax rate on the "sin" that exceeds the tax rate on general commodities. Sin taxation raises the price of sin, thereby discouraging it, as with alcohol and tobacco taxes in most economies. In contrast to prohibition, sin taxation keeps such goods legal and raises tax revenue.

Proponents of sin taxation rely on two arguments. First, that certain activities generate negative **externalities,** so policy should discourage consumption of these goods or services. For example, alcohol consumption can cause traffic fatalities, so policy should raise the price of alcohol to reduce its use. Second, that some consumers make irrational choices about consumption of the goods thought of as sins—consuming more than is good for them—so policy should discourage their use (see **paternalism**). For example, some drug users appear to be harming themselves, and raising the price might reduce this kind of behavior.

Sin taxation is a better policy than prohibition for addressing externalities or irrationality, but it generates several adverse side effects. Excessive sin taxation amounts to de facto prohibition, so it creates a black market and all the negative consequences. Sin taxes do not necessarily reach this level, but the risk is always present.

Even moderate sin taxes have unwanted effects. Sin taxes penalize those who can engage in drug use, prostitution, or gambling without hurting themselves or others, so the net impact on consumer welfare is ambiguous. The choice of which goods to regard as sins is not obvious and in practice reflects politics and morality more than good economics. Watching late-night TV, for example, might reduce productivity more than marijuana allegedly does, but demonizing marijuana users is easier politically than imposing a tax on late-night talk shows.

Similarly, designating some goods as sins might signal that people should not worry about the non-sins, but many of these, like an unhealthy diet, generate real harm. Following this reasoning, government could in fact start taxing a whole host of activities (see **slippery slopes**). Sin taxation also means that governments promote sin even while trying to discourage it (e.g., by banning private gambling while airing television ads that glamorize government lotteries).

Sin taxation, therefore, is not obviously better than treating all goods the same, even in the face of substantial negative externalities and individual irrationality. The one positive of sin taxation is that it might satisfy the public's demand to reduce the activities regarded as sins, thereby forestalling prohibition. This is especially likely when politicians want more tax revenue to spend.

See also **drug prohibition.**

slippery slopes

One defense of laissez-faire policies argues that interventions are unnecessary because markets work perfectly on their own. This view is not compelling, since market imperfections occur in many settings. Thus one can often make a case for intervention, which is why some economists are interventionists. We've seen many versions of this reasoning throughout other entries in this book.

A critical assumption behind the interventionist perspective, however, is that the intervention adopted is the right amount. Many people assume that because markets are imperfect, more intervention is always better. But interventions are often too large, which can be worse than no intervention at all. Ultra-strict emission controls on cars would make them so expensive that commerce would grind to a halt. Subsidizing education excessively encourages people to get degrees even when they would be better off getting a job. Too much redistribution discourages work and savings, shrinking the economic pie. The costs of taxation increase with the amount of revenue raised, so as government grows, this cost becomes increasingly important.

This issue is crucial because government programs do not always remain at the desirable level. All entities—individuals, firms, nonprofits, or government—attempt to survive, and one path to survival is getting bigger. Thus, once created, government agencies try to grow or expand their mission, and interventions that might make sense if small then become too large. This is especially problematic because government faces little competition, so bad performance is not readily driven out.

The historical record supports this view. Most government programs expand enormously and pursue activities much broader than their original mission. Indeed, few government policies or agencies have ever been eliminated or significantly scaled back.

Consider as illustration the Consumer Product Safety Commission, which among other duties verifies that toys are safe for children. Few would deny this is a worthy goal. Moreover, the intended beneficiaries cannot necessarily take care of themselves, and some parents neglect the safety of their children. Regulators must recognize, however, that making toys safer means making them more expensive; otherwise, manufacturers would do it on their own. Thus, regulators must choose an appropriate tradeoff between safety and cost.

Benevolent and omniscient regulators would choose the level of safety by balancing the welfare of children against the increased costs of toys. Real-world regulators, who consciously or subconsciously want to expand their mission, will perceive heightened dangers from toys because this means more toys to regulate. Real-world regulators will underestimate the effects of regulation on costs, again to increase the scope of their activities, and will go from low-cost interventions, like warning labels, to outright bans of particular toys.

Thus, while protecting child safety is a reasonable objective, and ideal regulators might nudge the private sector in a beneficial direction, actual regulators will almost certainly regulate too much.

This consideration applies generally. Civil rights legislation evolved from prohibitions against discrimination into affirmative action. The Pure Food and Drug Act went from requiring truthful disclosure of ingredients to banning many food substances and regulating the development and marketing of most medicines. Social Security grew from protecting the low-income elderly who could not work to providing retirement income to millionaires. Antitrust evolved from prohibiting monopolization to proscribing a large range of usually competitive practices, such as mergers between a manufacturing firm and one of its suppliers.

A different kind of overexpansion comes from policies that guarantee income or other benefits to particular subgroups of society. These entitlements are usually restricted on some basis such as income or age, which creates envy that can become acute when those who do not qualify are not particularly different from those who do. The creation of Medicare, which is health insurance for the elderly, at the same time as creation of Medicaid, which is health insurance for the poor, is a good example.

If excessive or undesirable policies were easy to fix, scale back, or eliminate, the problem of mission creep and overexpansion would not be overwhelming. But government programs are hard to eliminate, even if they work badly or become unnecessary. Most programs benefit some interest group, even if they harm society overall, and those interest groups will campaign to forestall sensible cuts with tales of lost jobs and other disastrous consequences. Knowing this will occur, societies should be wary of creating new government in the first place.

The tendency toward overexpansion is especially large because government often controls the information necessary to assess the program. A prime example is national security. The agencies in charge of protecting the country against terrorist threats would like the public to believe that they detect and prevent numerous attacks. At the same time, these agencies do not provide the information that would confirm the effectiveness of their efforts. The agencies have a possible reason for doing so: Providing details about foiled plots might compromise future security efforts. But their secrecy might also indicate that the number of foiled plots is small.

Social Security

The most common way governments provide retirement income is through Social Security programs. These levy taxes on the wage and salary income of the working-age population, accumulate these revenues in a trust fund, and pay benefits to persons who have contributed to this fund and reached a specified age. Early Social Security programs provided benefits only to people who had withdrawn from the labor force, but current programs allow people to work with small or zero reductions in benefits. Thus, Social Security payments are conditioned on reaching retirement age but not on retirement per se.

Advocates of Social Security programs rely on two arguments. First, that some people save too little for their own retirement—because they fail to consider the future consequences—and then find themselves impoverished in old age. Society, moreover, might not restrain itself from coming to the rescue of such persons after the fact, so it is allegedly better to avoid this temptation by guaranteeing retirement income in advance. The second argument maintains that some people earn too little during working years to build suitable retirement wealth, so society should help such people based on compassion.

Both arguments contain a grain of truth, but they do not make a strong case for Social Security. To begin with, the amount of old-age poverty that would occur without government is easily overstated. Living standards in developed countries are sufficiently high that households with moderate incomes can save enough for an acceptable if not luxurious nest egg. Families and private charities can and do support many of the low-income elderly. Private charity would be greater, moreover, if Social Security did not crowd it out. Additionally, the private sector would face increased incentive to provide financial instruments that facilitate retirement planning, like annuities or reverse mortgages, if Social Security did not reduce the demand for such innovations.

Thus the dismal picture painted by Social Security advocates, in which millions of elderly starve in the street, is a grotesque exaggeration. Elderly poverty has indeed declined over the past century, and while Social Security accounts for some of this, much of the decline reflects general improvements in living standards. In any case, Social Security imposes substantial costs on the economy.

A key cost is distortion of retirement behavior. Because benefits become available at a specific age, recipients have an incentive to retire at that age even if their earning ability is intact. Many elderly, however, can continue working or take less demanding jobs that replace some income. When Congress created Social Security, life expectancy at age 65 was substantially lower than today (as was average health status at age 65), so Social Security was insurance against outliving one's earnings ability. Because life expectancy has increased significantly, Social Security as it stands now encourages retirement for many who have not experienced a substantial decline in health or productivity.

A second cost of Social Security is reduced national savings. Because households operating under Social Security know they have guaranteed income in retirement, their incentive to save diminishes. Whether this impact of Social Security is large or small depends on more subtle issues, and the empirical evidence does not make an overwhelming case for such an effect.

Any impact in this direction, however, is a serious negative, since reduced savings means lower capital accumulation and therefore reduced economic growth.

Beyond these tangible effects, Social Security institutionalizes the notion that people cannot make good decisions for themselves. While some people do not plan for retirement, most would make a reasonable effort if they had to bear the full costs of inadequate saving. At the same time, policies that validate a lack of **self-reliance** can readily encourage such behavior.

Whatever the magnitude of elderly poverty that would exist without Social Security, and whether or not the costs of Social Security are large, a separate program to alleviate elderly poverty is unnecessary since a negative income tax can support both the low-income elderly and the low-income non-elderly. The integrated approach is likely less costly because it is explicitly anti-poverty and thus pays a low benefit, whereas Social Security raises benefits as the level of wages in the economy increases.

The alternative way to reduce Social Security's costs is to increase the retirement age—consistent with increases in life expectancy and health—and to freeze or reduce the level of benefits. This would return the program to its original intent: providing backup income to those who have outlived their ability to earn an income (i.e., disability insurance).

An additional, beneficial change in Social Security would eliminate Social Security taxes and the Trust Fund, instead paying benefits out of general tax revenues. This makes explicit that income support for the elderly could instead be income support for young children and the non-elderly disabled, or be spent on other government programs, or be left in the hands of taxpayers.

sports stadiums

Professional sports teams cannot earn a profit in small media markets, so many cities subsidize stadiums to attract these teams. The usual justification is that professional teams garner sufficient support from out-of-town fans to make these stadiums self-financing, through taxes on tickets, meals, and hotels. In addition, some people argue that sports like baseball are inherently American or support community values, implying their presence promotes some greater good.

Numerous studies, however, have refuted the claim that government funding for stadiums pays for itself. Most of the people who attend a local sporting event are locals. Thus they rarely utilize hotels to attend these sporting events, and their taxes do not bring new revenue into the city but instead represent a shift from some other activity.

The real reason for government funding of stadiums is that team owners and their buddies in the legislature get together to promote these projects, independent of the interests of the local citizens. The owners benefit financially, and the politicians get to watch sporting events as guests in the owner's luxury box. Local residents who do not enjoy having a local sports team end up subsidizing those who do.

See also **arts and culture.**

stabilization policies

Since the advent of Keynesian economics in the 1930s, most governments have attempted to dampen the business cycle of boom and bust using monetary and fiscal policies. These policies aim to promote economic stability, control inflation, and increase economic growth. No one doubts that capitalist economies experience business cycles, but the case for active stabilization is weak.

Stabilizing economies is difficult because monetary and fiscal policies operate with a lag. It takes time to recognize that an economy needs stimulus or restraint. It takes time to choose and implement a policy response. It takes time for policy to affect the economy. Lags would not be an issue if forecasting were easy and lags were predictable; then, policy could adjust in anticipation of upturns or downturns. In practice forecasting is inexact, and policy lags are "long and variable," as Milton Friedman emphasized. Thus attempts at stabilization can make the economy more volatile because sometimes policy stimulates or restrains when it should do the opposite.

Little evidence demonstrates that stabilization reduces economic volatility on average. The United States had no central bank before the founding of the Federal Reserve in 1914, yet economic growth was robust and the magnitude of the business cycle little different than in the decades under active stabilization policy. Individual states or provinces do not control their own monetary policy, yet their economies progress nonetheless. The countries of the European Union, and those that have tied their currencies to the dollar, Euro, or pound, have on average performed as well as those with independent monetary control. Both the **Great Depression** and the Financial

Crisis of 2008 resulted largely from government policy mistakes, not the failures of private markets.

A different problem with stabilization is that some fluctuations are plausibly beneficial for the economy over the long run. Rising oil prices are a sign the economy needs to invest in capital that can process alternative fuels, even though this might reduce growth in the short run. If a new technology like personal computers arrives, the economy might slow initially as it adapts.

Attempts at stabilization, moreover, have undesired effects. The private sector faces increased uncertainty because it must forecast policy rather than just forecasting the economy. Worse, instability can arise from the private sector's attempts to figure out what policy is going to do. The possibility that Congress might enact an investment tax credit, for example, encourages businesses to postpone investment so that these expenditures can later be eligible for the credit. An announcement that Treasury is going to purchase toxic assets from banks causes banks to freeze lending while they try to figure out how the purchase program might operate.

Preoccupation with short-run stability also diverts attention from long-run efficiency. Focus on stabilization, for example, might seem to legitimize inherently wasteful infrastructure projects to stimulate the economy (the classic example is paying workers to dig ditches and fill them up). Such policies hurt long-run growth, which has a far bigger impact on living standards than the fluctuations associated with business cycles.

subsidizing education

Many people view education as the means to a higher income, while others see it as a route to knowledge and understanding. All agree that education plays a key role in individual happiness and productivity, as well as in economic development. Moreover, virtually everyone believes that many people do not obtain the socially desirable amount of education on their own and that governments should therefore promote the appropriate quantity and kind.

Consistent with these views, governments subsidize education enormously. Cities and towns in the United States operate K–12 schools that offer free education to all residents. State governments operate colleges and universities at discounted tuition rates. State and federal governments award tuition subsidies, tax credits, and loans for higher education. Many governments run the entire educational system while charging little tuition at any level.

Government support of education is so pervasive that many people take it for granted. The fact that education can be productive or enjoyable, however, does not mean government should subsidize it. If education increases one's earnings potential, people can recognize this and acquire education on their own. If acquiring knowledge is pleasurable, individuals can do this for themselves. A convincing justification for subsidizing education must therefore argue that individuals collectively choose less education than is desirable for society overall.

Advocates of subsidy offer three reasons why the privately chosen level of education might be socially insufficient. First, society as a whole might benefit from an educated populace, beyond any benefit to the person acquiring the education. In economics language, education might generate "positive externalities"—spillovers that help others. For example, the ability to read, write, and use basic math might increase productivity of both the person acquiring these skills and the person's co-workers. Knowledge of standard accounting rules, computer programs, legal codes, or business practices might make a given employee more useful to other employees. More broadly, education might be civilizing, thereby promoting a peaceful and productive society.

The externality hypothesis is plausible, but it does not prove large education subsidies are desirable.

For starters, the mere *existence* of externalities does not determine the *magnitude* of externalities, and the amount of subsidy should depend on whether the externalities are quantitatively important. Much rhetoric, unfortunately, pretends that any increase in education subsidies is beneficial and any decrease disastrous. This may be the situation in poor countries, but it is far from obvious in rich countries.

Much subsidy, moreover, supports education for which the externalities are likely to be minimal. This includes education where recipients capture most of the full benefits in higher wages (e.g., business, law, medicine, computer science) and education where the impact on a recipient's income is minimal (e.g., philosophy, Sanskrit).

Externalities are also difficult to measure and often exist only in the eye of the beholder. People who like the humanities think they are civilizing. People who like science believe it generates important new technologies that benefit everyone. People who like economics find its insights critical to sensible policy making. These views may have merit, but they are easily exaggerated to justify education that does not generate substantial externalities.

The second possible justification for subsidizing education is based on **paternalism**. According to this view, some people fail to recognize that education can increase their income by more than its costs. These people therefore purchase too little, even from their own perspective. In particular, some parents might purchase insufficient education for their children unless policy keeps the cost of education low.

While paternalism seems reasonable, it opens a Pandora's box of government intervention. The same argument that suggests protecting people from themselves by encouraging education can also suggest encouraging or discouraging religion, encouraging or discouraging sports, and banning or requiring certain books, ideas, and schools. Even worse, paternalism can hurt precisely those it aims to help. People who are shortsighted might be worse than average at recognizing the opportunity costs of education or the forgone wages, or they might overestimate the income-enhancing effect of education. So, lowering the explicit cost could cause these people to purchase too much education rather than too little.

A different problem with paternalism is that parents can make numerous poor choices for their children: providing inadequate medical care, allowing too much TV, or creating excessive pressure to excel in sports. Thus bad parental choices about a child's education might be almost irrelevant given a large number of other mistakes.

The third argument for subsidizing education is that some people cannot afford it. This view is correct but easily overstated. Families in middle- and upper-income communities are already paying substantial amounts for education in the form of property taxes. Banks make loans for education. Schools and private foundations grant loans or scholarships. Apprenticeships allow unskilled workers to obtain training by accepting initially low wages, a practice that would likely be more common were it not for **minimum-wage** laws, compulsory schooling, and minimum work ages. Attending school part-time, or borrowing from family and friends, diminishes the impact of low income.

The benefits from subsidizing education are thus not necessarily large. Subsidizing education also has adverse side effects.

The first negative is that if government subsidizes education, it must define education. If the subsidy comes in the form of public schools, government must choose curricula, set standards for hiring teachers, and so on. If the subsidy comes as loans or scholarships, government must decide what kinds of instruction these can purchase. Imposing one kind of education fails to recognize that while some students benefit from standard curricula, others get more out of schools focused on science, foreign languages, the arts, vocational training, or sports.

Subsidizing education also entangles government in divisive issues. All schools must take a stand, for example, on whether to teach evolution or creationism, on whether to have dress or speech codes, on what to do if a professor teaches offensive material, and on whether to practice affirmative action in admissions or hiring. For a government-supported school, taking either side generates controversy because it forces taxpayers to support positions they dislike. For a private school, this issue does not arise because no one is required to attend that school.

Government definition and control of education also promotes certain ideas relative to others: that democracy is good, that capitalism needs regulation, that separating church and state is desirable, that recycling helps the environment. Whatever the merits of these particular positions, it is inevitable that government involvement tilts the intellectual landscape.

None of these negatives proves that the right amount of education subsidy is zero. Since the case for subsidy is not overwhelming, however, and since subsidizing education has its own negatives, the appropriate subsidy is far lower than in most economies, and perhaps zero. At a minimum, the subsidy should focus on children who might not otherwise get an education, and on education that generates externalities. This is unlikely to include, for example, reduced tuition for middle-class kids getting college degrees, professional degrees, or Ph.D.s in comparative literature.

A different question is which level of government should set education policy, if government intervenes at all. The ideal is to leave education to the most local level of government, rather than to a federal or national government. All the issues of **polarization**, excessive standardization, lack of competition, and so on are greater if a centralized government sets education policy than if fifty states or, better yet, thousands of cities and towns have autonomy to experiment and compete in response to the needs of their communities.

taxes

Even small governments require some expenditure, so taxes are necessary in every society. At the same time, taxes impose costs, so it important to keep taxes low and to design tax systems that do minimal damage.

Taxes are costly for society because they distort economic decisions. In the absence of taxes on wage and salary income, for example, each individual chooses an amount of work such that the extra amount earned is sufficient to compensate for the loss of leisure time. In the presence of taxes on income, however, the incentive to work is reduced because the earner does not keep all the fruits of his labor; taxes introduce a wedge between the effort and the reward obtained, thus discouraging effort. Similar considerations apply to taxes on interest or dividend income, which discourage saving, or taxes on specific goods and services, which cause substitutions to other goods that are not driven by differences in the cost of producing those goods.

It is possible to design non-distorting taxes. A lump-sum assessment—one that is the same independent of taxpayer behavior—does not distort behavior. The standard example is a head tax: everyone pays, say, $10,000 in taxes. Most societies do not seem to regard such taxes as fair, however, so they are rarely employed.

Taxes also generate compliance costs. Individuals spend time filling out forms or pay others to do it for them. Businesses expend resources collecting and processing sales and employment taxes. Corporations must compute and comply with the corporate income tax. All these entities expend further effort avoiding or evading taxation.

The implication of these costs is that government expenditure of a dollar costs the economy more than a dollar, given the necessity of paying for the expenditure with distorting taxes. Thus, even interventions with benefits in excess of direct costs might not be desirable; the benefits must also outweigh the tax distortions and compliance costs that will result from the taxation needed to pay those direct costs.

The costs generated by taxes do not by themselves mean government expenditure is undesirable, but they need to be recognized in any honest analysis. For some policies, including much of the government's regulatory efforts, the implied tax costs are modest since the expenditure for these policies is modest. For other policies, such as transfer programs like Social Security, Medicare, Medicaid, and Disability Insurance, the implied tax costs are substantial because expenditure on these programs is substantial.

In practice most tax systems do far more harm than necessary. This is because modern tax systems do not just raise revenue but also promote goals like homeownership or alternative energy, and they attempt to redistribute income from richer to poorer. This generates far greater economic distortion and compliance costs than if governments simply raised revenue in the least distorting manner.

Tax reforms attempt to reduce these unnecessary costs of the tax system while holding revenue constant. Numerous modifications make sense, but the political reality is that significant improvement is unlikely without a substantial reduction in expenditure. So long as governments have major revenue needs, it is difficult to engineer beneficial changes in the structure since any reduction in revenue must be offset by an increase elsewhere. Thus while reform of the tax code is a worthy goal, reduced expenditure is more important yet since this is a precondition of significant reform.

thought control

A widespread consequence of government intervention is limiting ideas, inhibiting free expression, and pushing some views at the expense of others. In extreme cases this thought control is obvious—such as when a government outlaws particular religions or political parties—but the scope for policy to limit ideas is much broader.

The potential for thought control is greatest for policy areas like education, where government explicitly decides that some curricula, textbooks, methods of teaching, programs of study, and so on are more deserving than others. Similarly, when government funds research, it explicitly passes judgment on what ideas are worthy and which are less so. Even policies that are not directly related to ideas, however, implicitly support certain "correct" views of the world. Economic regulation takes a stand on how markets work; taxing corporations perpetuates a view that inanimate objects, not people, pay taxes; redistributing income takes a position on self-reliance; campaign finance regulation and estate taxation endorse particular views of wealth.

Thus government cannot intervene without endorsing particular ideas about how society should be run, about who should be the winners and losers, and about what is good or bad. If this were implemented by benevolent, competent people, the negatives might be small, but that is not the way the world works. People are imperfect. Some policy makers do not have good intentions, and those who do make mistakes. So putting control over ideas into the hands of a few is fraught with potential for disaster.

Many regard this last point as ridiculous exaggeration; they see no evidence that countries like the United States are slipping toward George Orwell's *1984*. Yet modern governments intervene far more than they have in the past, and people have come to accept a larger and larger role for government, affecting every aspect of economic and social life. Everyone can identify certain areas, moreover, where in their opinion governments intervene too much (e.g., foreign policy for liberals, economic regulation for conservatives). Thus everyone should accept that governments do not always act benevolently and that undesirable actions in one arena might pave the way for future worse behavior. This does not by itself mean small, well-designed interventions are undesirable, but it adds yet one more reason for caution.

too big to fail

During numerous episodes of financial turmoil, governments have "bailed out" the banking sector when investment losses threatened the viability of its largest institutions. Most recently, the U.S. Treasury's Troubled Asset Relief Program (TARP) provided hundreds of billions of dollars to the banking and financial sectors during the Financial Crisis of 2008.

The standard justification for bailing out banks—rather than letting them go bankrupt, which is what happens in other sectors—holds that the largest banks are "too big to fail" because their demise would adversely affect the entire credit system.

That is, the assumption is that failure by some banks would harm the overall economy, rather than just transmitting whatever negative shock has already hit the bank stockholders, creditors, and counterparties. This negative **externality** from a bank failure might occur in part because a bank has unique abilities to make productive loans that cannot be easily supplied by other lenders in the short term. The negative externality might also occur because failure by one bank could precipitate failure of other, healthy banks that have lent money to the failing bank.

The view that bank failures can generate credit crises is understandable and perhaps right in some measure. Nevertheless, bailouts and too-big-to-fail are bad policies.

To see why, note first that when a bank faces bankruptcy, it does not simply disappear. Instead, a federal regulator takes over the bank, resolves the claims against it, and sells off what remains. Shareholders of the failing bank lose their stake, and creditors often take a substantial loss. The remaining bank is then either sold wholesale to a healthy bank, or carved up into pieces and its assets sold to various parties. Taxpayer funds go at most to insured depositors.

The question, then, is how bailout compares to bankruptcy from three perspectives: the impact on the distribution of wealth, the impact on economic efficiency in the long run, and the impact on the length and depth of financial disruption in the short run.

From a distributional perspective, bailout is unambiguously perverse: It transfers resources from the general taxpayer to well-off economic actors who profited from risky investments. This is not a criticism of risk taking, which is appropriate so long as those benefiting in good times bear the costs in bad times. This is exactly what occurs under bankruptcy.

From an efficiency perspective, bailout is again problematic because it creates a **moral hazard**. Bailout not only transfers resources to those who took excessive risks; by so doing, it creates an incentive to take excessive risks in future. Following this logic, every bailout plants the seeds of an even greater financial crisis down the line. Because bailouts do not force large institutions to fail, moreover, they perpetuate exactly the kind of institutions that might appear too big to fail. The long-run consequences of bailout are thus inferior to those of bankruptcy.

Bailout is superior to bankruptcy, therefore, only if allowing bank failures would cause adverse effects in the short run—a recession—that outweigh the negative distributional and long-run consequences of bailouts.

Neither theory nor evidence, however, makes a convincing case that bank failures generate additional negative impacts on the economy, rather than just revealing the underlying mis-allocations that prompted failures in the first place. As a theoretical matter, failure by a bank means that it cannot extend credit, but this implies a profitable lending opportunity for someone else. Relatedly, any special talent a particular bank has for making loans is likely to reside in the people who worked there, and these same people can work for other banks or lenders. As an empirical matter, the evidence that failures cause additional harm, rather than just reflecting harm that has already occurred, is weak.

This is not to deny that credit freezes occur and cause harm. Rather, the claim is that financial crises arise in part because the private sector has invested excessively in some aspect of the economy (in 2008 it was housing, but in other episodes it has been commercial real estate, or stocks) and that therefore an economic adjustment was needed to restore reasonable balance. This can only happen via a recession.

Thus too-big-to-fail has huge potential for counterproductive impacts and at best an uncertain prospect of alleviating credit crunches or ameliorating recessions. This means policy should allow banks to fail no matter how large. This creates better incentives going forward for private behavior toward risk. The short-term adjustment to bank failures might be messy, but that is a price worth paying.

trade

The free exchange of goods and services between nations is one of the most important sources of economic gain. No country can produce everything, let alone produce everything in an efficient manner. Free trade allows each country to specialize in the production of the goods it produces well while permitting its residents to choose from the maximum possible set of goods, at the lowest possible prices. An unambiguous commitment to free trade is thus perhaps the single most important economic policy that any nation can adopt.

Despite the abundant benefits of free trade, all countries impose some trade restrictions and many impose substantial barriers. These take many forms: tariffs (taxes on imported goods), quotas (limits on the amount of imports), voluntary export restraints, and export subsidies, plus more subtle measures such as non-trade regulation that mainly aims to block competition for a domestically produced product (e.g., certain environmental rules). All of these policies are bad for the country imposing them and bad for the rest of the world—yet they remain attractive to a wide swath of interest groups and so garner support from many politicians.

One way a country can promote free trade is by entering multilateral trade agreements, such as the North American Free Trade Agreement, or by joining international organizations like the World Trade Organization. These approaches are fine as far as they go, but a better approach is for a country to eliminate all its trade barriers unilaterally. This provides immediate benefits to consumers and the competitive environment, as opposed to the huge delays that accompany multilateral bargaining.

unintended consequences

No matter how well-intentioned, most interventions have unintended consequences that end up causing more harm than any problem the policy was designed to fix. Many of these consequences, moreover, could not have been forecast at the time the policy was enacted. This truism provides a crucial foundation for the libertarian point of view.

In 1914, when the United States began prohibiting drugs, no one could have predicted that AIDS would emerge more than a half-century later. Yet, because the elevated prices caused by prohibition encourage drug injection (since this gives a big bang for the buck), the prohibition-fostered restrictions on clean needles have led to sharing of contaminated syringes, thereby spreading HIV.

When Congress created Social Security in 1935, life expectancy was roughly 65, and many elderly suffered reduced health and productivity well before this age. Social Security was therefore mainly income support for those who could not provide for themselves in old age. Nowadays many people live past 65 in reasonable health, and this creates the expectation that everyone deserves a comfortable retirement. This expectation is not by itself a problem, except that many people assume taxpayers should foot the bill.

When Congress created the National Institutes of Health, no one could have anticipated that stem cell research would create controversy associated with federal funding. As the result of this controversy, strong pressure ensued for a federal ban on stem cell research, even if conducted with private funds. So far a ban has not occurred, but federal funding increased the likelihood of such an outcome.

When Congress created the Medicaid program of health insurance for the poor, few predicted that the Supreme Court's *Roe v. Wade* decision would raise the question of whether Medicaid funds should pay for abortions—a question that generates animosity to this day.

The U.S. entry into World War I contributed to the harsh treatment of postwar Germany by the Allies, which fostered the environment in which Nazism arose. U.S. participation in the war allowed it to insert in the Treaty of Versailles a requirement that all signatories adopt drug prohibition.

During World War II, the United States imposed wage and price controls. In response, businesses offered health insurance as a way to compensate employees without violating the controls. This is one reason insurance now comes from employers. The key negative is that many employees feel locked into their existing jobs.

Creation of the Food and Drug Administration was meant to protect the public from unsafe drugs. Most liberals support the FDA, regarding markets as an insufficient mechanism for preventing bad drugs. Yet this same agency played a key role in delaying the availability of **RU-486**, the abortion pill, which would have aided precisely the constituency supported by these same liberals.

The creation by Congress of the Federal National Mortgage Association (Fannie Mae) in 1938 and of the Federal Home Loan Mortgage Corporation (Freddie Mac) in 1968 was intended to increase homeownership by fostering a secondary market in mortgage securities, thereby lowering mortgage interest rates because of reduced risk. No one anticipated that political and economic pressures would cause provision of these loans to large numbers of borrowers with weak credit histories, nor that decades later housing prices would boom (which covered up the fact that many mortgage loans were problematic) and then decline substantially (which exposed many borrowers' inability to pay). Many people did not acknowledge that government sponsorship of these enterprises meant that government was, in effect, guaranteeing the mortgage-backed securities issued by Fannie and Freddie. Yet the extension of problematic loans and the housing price shock occurred, leading to the serious financial disruption and government bailouts of affected institutions that the United States experienced in 2008 and 2009.

These examples might seem extreme, but the tendency for intervention to change incentives is pervasive. Rent control lowers the return to building apartments and therefore reduces the supply of housing. The **Endangered Species** Act encourages preemptive destruction of habitats that might contain endangered species. Anti-discrimination laws encourage firms to avoid hiring members of protected groups so they cannot be sued for firing them. **Union** protections encourage businesses to relocate overseas, generating even lower wages for employees in the original country. **Agricultural subsidies** encourage overuse of water and pesticides.

All this happens because interventions change incentives, sometimes in ways that are hard to predict. The fact that the future is uncertain is not necessarily a reason for inaction. Yet when government introduces something new, it risks setting into motion these unintended consequences. Rational evaluation should recognize that the devil one knows might be better than the devil one has not yet met.

unions

Most governments protect unions. That is, they pursue policies that push employers to negotiate with unions and to agree on compensation packages that are more generous than would occur without these protections. In the United States pro-union policies are relatively mild, consisting mainly of the requirement that employers bargain in good faith and allow unions to organize on their property. In other countries union protections are much stronger, including bans on replacement workers, bans on plant shutdowns, and restrictions on plant relocations.

The standard justification for protecting unions is the desire to raise the wages of union employees. This makes no sense from the perspective of economic efficiency. Artificially raising the price of union labor encourages firms to utilize alternative production techniques (e.g., ones involving more automation and less labor) or to move their factories to countries with lower wages.

The only possible defense of union protections, therefore, is the redistribution of wealth, but the distributional implications of union protections are bizarre. These provide higher wages for those who get union jobs, while they lower overall employment. Thus union members are better off, but those who do not get union jobs are worse off. This is an odd way to redistribute income.

These objections to government protections for unions are not a criticism of unions per se. If the employees of a given firm or industry wish to organize and attempt to bargain collectively with their employers, that is their choice. Stated differently, the problem is not unions but the government policies that alter the bargaining power between employers and unions. In a world with no government protections for unions, some might still exist because employers would find it convenient to bargain collectively. The degree to which unions could raise wages, however, would be substantially smaller.

utilitarianism

The utilitarian perspective on policy argues that any economic allocation provides a certain amount of happiness—utility—to each person and that policy should seek to maximize aggregate happiness. In particular, the utilitarian view assumes that the utility associated with any amount of individual wealth declines as the level of wealth increases, so an additional bit of income means more to a poor person than to a rich person.

The utilitarian assumption is plausible in many cases, but re-distribution based on the utilitarian perspective is problematic because it sets an unfortunate precedent. If government can decree that poor people are more deserving than rich people, then government can decree that certain races, religions, ages, genders, or political views are more deserving as well—all based on utilitarian principles.

The one act does not inevitably generate the other, but making distinctions between groups is the first step down a **slippery slope**. Indeed, many governments have targeted or suppressed specific groups based on the explicit or implicit assertion that some groups are more deserving than others. Examples include Nazi Germany's treatment of the Jews, Stalin's purges of non-communists, the U.S. internment of Americans of Japanese descent during World War II, South Africa's treatment of blacks under apartheid, Jim Crow laws in the U.S. South, or the Tuskegee syphilis experiments on African-Americans. Even if some kinds of differential treatment seem reasonable—asking billionaires to pay higher tax rates than those near poverty—the way to avoid slipping into inappropriate kinds of differential treatment is to avoid any precedent for such an approach.

vouchers for education

The main way that most governments **subsidize education** is by owning and operating public schools. These institutions are typically open to everyone who lives in a specified area; tuition is free or substantially reduced.

An alternative way to subsidize education is vouchers. Under this policy, parents of school-age children receive a piece of paper—the voucher—that can be used to purchase education at any institution. Private schools accept vouchers as payment because a government entity promises to redeem the vouchers for money. The voucher amount need not equal the cost of an education at every school. If a basic K–12 education costs $3,000 a year, the voucher might be $3,000 so that all families could purchase this package. Some schools might charge more, however, and parents with sufficient income would pay the differential from their own resources.

Vouchers are a better way to subsidize than public schools. Under vouchers, all schools are private and therefore have the freedom and incentive to supply variety and innovation; likewise, private schools face incentives to control costs, such as teacher salaries, and oppose regulation that raises costs unnecessarily, such as certification rules for teachers that do not generate quality teaching. Under vouchers it is easier, although not easy, to address controversial issues such as single-sex schools, speech codes, faculty with inflammatory political views, and affirmative action; governments can simply accept vouchers from a broad range of schools, subject to minimal conditions about quality, without taking an explicit stand on such policies.

Existing evidence suggests vouchers produce better educational outcomes than public schools, although not to a dramatic degree. Claims that vouchers produce a radical improvement in the quality of education are not substantiated by evidence and don't necessarily follow from logic. But vouchers do produce increased consumer satisfaction. When public or private groups offer vouchers or access to charter schools, demand routinely exceeds supply, even when objective measures like test scores do not show great improvement relative to public schools. The increased satisfaction that parents and students obtain is an important benefit of vouchers; improvements in quantifiable outcomes like test scores or graduation rates are desirable but not the only valid objective.

Another advantage of vouchers is lower costs of producing education. Private schools are not bound by the union contracts that set salaries in public schools, and private sector teachers' unions face much greater obstacles in bargaining collectively. As a result, private schools do not face a large union wage premium in teacher salaries. Similarly, private schools do not face other constraints imposed by current regulation, like requirements to hire certified teachers. Reducing costs is an advantage of the voucher approach, even if vouchers have no impact on test scores or other indicators of academic achievement, since the resources saved are available for other uses.

A potential concern about vouchers is that they permit de facto segregation by race, ethnicity, religion, or income. This concern is misplaced, whether or not policy should promote diversity. On the one hand, segregation by race, income, and so on already occurs—indeed, is extreme—in many neighborhood public schools. On the other hand, many people choose diverse schools when free to do so, and private high schools, colleges, and universities offer scholarships for minorities and practice **affirmative action** in admissions. Thus diversity would not necessarily decline under vouchers and might even increase.

The ideal voucher system would replace public schools entirely. Every student would get a voucher to attend a private school. This approach circumvents the objection that vouchers are a back-door way of eliminating public schools, since it makes explicit that this is precisely the objective. Alternatively, vouchers could be provided only to low-income students. This might be a reasonable way to redistribute income, but that is a separate question from whether to employ vouchers or public schools.

vouchers versus redistribution in-cash or in-kind

Government-operated anti-poverty programs can provide income transfers either in-cash or in-kind. "In-cash" means recipients get money that can be spent on whatever goods and services the recipients desire. "In-kind" means recipients get specific goods, such as free vaccinations, meals at soup kitchens, medical care, government housing, or public schools. In this case recipients must "purchase" not only the kind of good being supplied by the government but also the specific version, e.g., the particular public school or housing project. In between income-in-cash transfers and income-in-kind transfers are vouchers, pieces of paper that can be redeemed for specific categories of goods such as food, education, or housing. In this case recipients must purchase a particular kind of good, but they retain flexibility about the exact version and can purchase from private suppliers.

Cash transfers are normally better than vouchers, and vouchers better than in-kind transfers. Cash gives recipients the most choice about how to spend the income received, which is valuable because the right mix of expenditure often varies across transfer recipients. Some households need good schools, others transportation to a job, still others medical care, and so on. Assuming recipients make reasonable expenditure decisions, therefore, cash maximizes the well-being of recipients for any given amount of income transferred.

If recipients do not make reasonable choices, then constraining the goods on which transfers are spent might increase their welfare. A standard concern, for example, is that some recipients might spend cash transfers on alcohol, drugs, or gambling.

This concern is a reason to consider vouchers, which constrain purchases to a particular kind of good but allow choice within that category. Housing vouchers, for example, force recipients to spend that transfer on housing but allow the transfer to be used in any neighborhood, not just at a government housing project in an inner-city slum. Vouchers are better than direct government provision because they leave production to the private sector, which is more efficient. Vouchers also permit choice regarding the private provider of the product. At the same time, vouchers pose little risk of serious misuse. One can spend an education voucher on a mediocre school, but one cannot easily gamble it away at the race track.

The choice between cash and vouchers is not as clear cut. Cash allows recipients to make bad choices about how they spend their transfers, but this might be an acceptable risk for policy to take since the extra choice benefits some recipients.

Some of those inclined to make bad use of a cash transfer will do so even with a voucher, either by cashing out the voucher in a black market or by using it to purchase inferior-quality goods. Cash is also less paternalistic, and cash prevents political forces from tilting the uses of vouchers.

For a few goods, vouchers might be preferable to cash. The obvious examples are education and health, especially for young children. Although most parents make reasonable choices for their children, some will use cash transfers for inappropriate purposes. Nudging such parents to spend their transfers on goods like education and vaccinations might provide a lower bound on how bad a given child's circumstances can be.

war on terror

Many countries, and especially the United States, expend substantial resources to fight terrorism and promote domestic security. The magnitude and scope of these efforts expanded noticeably after 9/11, but they have been significant in other times and places (e.g., attempts by the United States to eliminate communists from government during the 1950s). These efforts are enormously costly, rarely effective at promoting security or fighting terrorism, and potentially counterproductive.

The fundamental problem is that the war on terror embodies a flawed view of why individuals or groups perpetrate terrorist acts. The image conjured up is that of madmen whose hatred of the United States pushes them to commit violent attacks on innocents, with no expectation these might achieve any specific goal. In other words, terrorists' allegedly aim merely to terrorize, rather than to achieve a specific military or political objective. This perspective is almost totally wrong.

The vast majority of those who sponsor or commit terrorism have specific political goals. The rebels in Chechnya want independence from Russia. The Basque separatists want independence from Spain. The Kashmiri fighters want to separate from India. The drug lords in Colombia want to intimidate the government into refusing extradition of drug prisoners to the United States. The Palestinians want the return of Palestine, while Islamic fundamentalists want the United States out of the Middle East. The Irish Republican Army wants Northern Ireland to be independent from the United Kingdom. The most famous domestic terrorist—Timothy McVeigh—fits the madman stereotype better than all but a handful of foreign terrorists, yet even he had a political motive (the building he bombed was owned and occupied by the federal government).

While the tactics employed by so-called terrorists are frightening because they target civilians, much terrorism is just warfare by groups that cannot wage conventional war because of their limited size and resources.

In addition, terrorism sometimes achieves the objectives of the terrorists. For example, the Peace Now movement in Israel, which advocates ceding land for peace, obtains some of its support from Israelis weary with suicide bombings and other attacks on Israel. The electoral defeat of a pro-Bush government in Spain resulted in part from bomb attacks on the Madrid train system. Terrorist attacks often fail, but the groups in question are fighting uphill battles to begin with. None of this means terrorists are right, but they are typically acting rationally, given their objectives.

This perspective has two implications. First, a global war on terror makes no sense. The issues in dispute vary from country to country, and most do not concern the United States. Second, the way to reduce some kinds of terrorism is to give the terrorists what they want, since the demand for terrorism results from excessive government that should be scaled back in any case. Russia might give Chechnya greater independence; India might cede Kashmir to Pakistan; Turkey might allow Muslims greater religious freedom or Kurds greater autonomy. Yielding to terrorist demands does not make sense in all cases, but it deserves rational consideration.

A critical question is what policy change would reduce the number of terrorist acts against the United States. The single most important is elimination of U.S. support for Israel and termination of any U.S. presence in the Middle East. These interventions are expensive and have no convincing justification. (For example, the threat that the United States would not have access to oil is vastly overstated since Middle East countries have little choice but to sell their oil on the world market.) Worse, these interventions generate antipathy toward the United States and do not obviously increase the welfare of Jews or others in the Middle East (unrestricted immigration would be far more effective). Much evidence indicates that the overriding concern of Muslim fundamentalists is control of the Middle East, rather than general opposition to the United States.

Another, equally troubling aspect of the war on terror is specific security measures such as passenger screening at airports. These are a huge waste of resources. Independent audits routinely find ways to beat these systems, and terrorists have countless other targets like subways, trains, sports stadiums, and bridges. Other anti-terrorism tactics, such as aggressive questioning of enemy combatants, warrantless wiretaps, or unlimited detentions without access to counsel, are ill-advised not just because they raise civil liberty concerns but because little evidence suggests they reduce terrorism. Thus most security and anti-terrorism efforts create lots of costs with minimal demonstrable benefits.

Politicians and the media repeatedly assert that drug trafficking causes terrorism, based on the co-occurrence of these phenomena in countries like Colombia, Peru, or Afghanistan. Drug trafficking and terrorism are related, but the link is drug prohibition. Drug trafficking generates income while terrorism does not; drug traffickers need protection, which terrorists can provide assuming they have money to buy guns. So traffickers hire terrorist groups to protect the drug trade from law enforcement.

If drugs were legal, profits would be no higher than in any other industry, and terrorists would struggle to find other sources of income. Law enforcement could reallocate resources from anti-drug enforcement to fighting terrorists. Thus, the way to reduce terrorism in drug-producing countries is to legalize drugs.

ZOOS

See **arts and culture** *and* **sports stadiums.**

the intellectual foundations of the libertarian perspective

This book is not the place for a detailed discussion of the intellectual antecedents of the libertarian perspective presented here. Many readers may nevertheless appreciate a brief primer on the most important earlier libertarians and their intellectual predecessors, the classical liberals. Readers interested in a fuller understanding of the history and philosophy of libertarianism should consult David Boaz's *Libertarianism: A Primer*, from which this entry cribs shamelessly.

John Locke (1632–1704) was an English physician and philosopher. In his *Second Treatise on Government* (1689), he argued that people have natural rights, such as ownership of property, and that the sole purpose of government is to safeguard these natural rights.

Adam Smith (1723–1790) was a Scottish moral philosopher and political economist. In *The Wealth of Nations* (1776), he gave an early and eloquent defense of laissez-faire capitalism, explaining how individual, self-motivated actions could, as if led by an "invisible hand," generate prosperity for the many. According to Smith, these decentralized decisions produce a "spontaneous order" in which the actions of individual consumers and businesses end up being coordinated in markets or other private arrangements, without the need for government intervention. Arguably, Locke's theory of individual rights and limited government and Smith's description of the market are the foundations of modern society.

Jeremy Bentham (1748–1832) was an English jurist and philosopher known for the theory of **utilitarianism**: the view that policy should attempt to produce "the greatest good for the greatest number of people." This view sounds similar to the **consequential libertarian** perspective, and in broad-brush terms it is. Some modern advocates of utilitarianism, however, support views on income inequality that libertarians do not share (see **redistribution**).

John Stuart Mill (1806–1873) was an English philosopher and student of Bentham's, as well as a proponent of utilitarianism. In *On Liberty* (1869), he defended the right of individuals to control their own mind and body and argued that the only appropriate exercise of power is to prevent individuals from harming others.

Ludvig von Mises (1881–1973) was an Austrian economist who argued in *Socialism* (1922) that that system was inimical to economic progress because government planners could never hope to make the intricate calculations required to allocate all the goods in a modern economy. Relatedly, he emphasized that the price signals generated by a capitalist economy would promote an efficient allocation. Mises also warned that expansions of credit by governments would generate boom and bust cycles.

F. A. Hayek (1899–1992) was another Austrian economist and a student of Mises. In *The Road to Serfdom* (1944) Hayek argued that socialism did not merely give government power over economic matters, which was already undesirable given general government incompetence at managing complex tasks, but that such powers implied control over personal freedoms as well, facilitating the march toward totalitarian states like Nazi Germany or Communist Russia.

Robert Nozick (1938–2002) was an American philosophy professor at Harvard University. In *Anarchy, State, and Utopia* (1974), Nozick sought to refute John Rawls's view in *A Theory of Justice* (1971) that government should redistribute income to protect the least fortunate members of society. Based on a theory of natural rights, Nozick argued that redistribution is not a legitimate function of government, which should limit itself to enforcing property rights and contracts.

Ayn Rand (1905–1982) was a Russian-born novelist and philosopher. Her two novels *The Fountainhead* (1943) and especially *Atlas Shrugged* (1957) achieved an enormous popular following and introduced many outside academia to the libertarian political philosophy espoused in these books. Rand insisted she was not a libertarian (she used the term Objectivist for her views), but her conclusions about policy were identical to those of libertarians. Her arguments were decidedly rights-based, rather than consequentialist, and not always appealing to economists because they feel more like assertion or religion than logic or science.

Milton Friedman (1912–2006) was an American economist who advocated free-market principles and small government based on a consequential rather than a philosophical approach. His columns in *Newsweek* addressed the ongoing economic and political debates of the day, while his *Capitalism and Freedom* (1962) argued for free-market policies and emphasized that economic freedoms are as important as, and necessary for, political freedoms.

The prior work that most closely resembles the approach taken here is that by the economists—Smith, Mises, Hayek, and especially Friedman, all of whose arguments for limited government are explicitly consequentialist rather than rights-based. As I and many others have suggested, the conflict between rights-based and consequential defenses of small government is more apparent than real, but the arguments presented by some rights-based libertarians can seem difficult to evaluate because they start from assertions that are not readily amenable to analysis or empirical examination (e.g., Rand's statement, in a famous *Playboy* interview by Alvin Toffler, that "The Objectivist ethics, in essence, hold that man exists for his own sake, that the pursuit of his own happiness is his highest moral purpose, that he must not sacrifice himself to others, nor sacrifice others to himself").

Yet it is wrong to think of philosophical versus consequential arguments for libertarian conclusions as antagonistic; rather, in my view, they are different languages or descriptions of the same ideas and reasoning: Whether one argues that the goal of government is protecting individual rights or promoting policies with the greatest ratio of costs to benefits, the answer turns out to be similar. This similarity of conclusions suggests immediately that the rights-based and consequential approaches are on some level the same, just as a geometric proof and an algebraic proof of a particular math theorem must both be correct, assuming the theorem is true.

conclusion

It is human nature, perhaps, to hope that every problem has a solution. In the policy arena, this means believing government can fix whatever is wrong with the economy or society.

The consequential libertarian perspective holds that this viewpoint is naïve. Even though markets are not perfect, governments usually make things worse. This reality seems harsh, so many people want to believe that government can find a remedy for whatever is wrong with society or the economy.

If the analysis here is correct, however, the search for ideal solutions is misguided. In the policy arena, as in other aspects of life, the best can be the enemy of the good. Laissez-faire is not perfect, but it is still the right choice if non-intervention is less bad than the available interventions. This view is not an easy sell for politicians, or for much of the public, yet it is indisputable. Policy makers and society cannot choose between non-intervention and hypothetical, ideal interventions. We must always choose between non-intervention, with all its limitations, and actual interventions, with all their imperfections.

One common response to the conclusions offered here is, "You may be right on the merits, but it's politically impossible to adopt the policies you propose." This is an understandable point of view, since few of the policy changes recommended in this book are likely to occur soon. It might seem, therefore, that compromise is the only road to better policies.

In accepting compromise, however, it is crucial to understand what the best policy would be so that compromises are in the right direction. Otherwise, the tendency is to fix bad government with yet more government. Advocates of small government can rightly push for policy changes that, if not optimal, at least scale back government somewhat. But they should never accept policies that they would normally oppose, except for the desire to "do something." That is the road we have traveled for too long. It is time to stand up for what we believe.